Problem Solving
BOOK B

MATH AT HAND

GReaT SouRCe®

EDUCATION GROUP
A Houghton Mifflin Company
New Ways to Know®

Developing

thinking skills through

READING and **WRITING**

Credits

Writing: Justine Dunn, Judy Vandegrift

Review: Ed Manfre

Editorial: Carol DeBold, Pearl Ling, Susan Rogalski

Design/Production: Taurins Design

Creative Art: Alex Farquharson *pages 8, 10, 11, 14 (bottom), 24 (bottom), 29, 44, 46, 51, 81, 85*. Greg Harris *pages 49, 73, 76, 77*. Amanda Harvey *page 38*. Eileen Hine *icons*. Steve Mach *pages 72, 80*. Stacey Schuett *page iv*. Susan Spellman *pages 2, 4, 6, 14 (top right), 20, 23, 24 (top), 32, 92, 93, 94, 96, 98, 99, 100*.

Technical Art: Taurins Design

Photos: Corbis *pages iv, 1 (top), 3 (bottom), 7, 10, 13 (bottom), 18, 19, 22, 26, 28, 29, 30, 36, 37, 40, 54 (background), 55 (top right), 60, 72, 73, 74, 83, 84, 87, 90, 91 (top left & bottom left), 93*. Greg Chann *page 47*. The 5,000-Year-Old Puzzle: Solving a Mystery of Ancient Egypt © 2002 by Claudia Logan, pictures by Melissa Sweet. Used with the permission of Farrar, Strauss & Giroux *page 9*. Kenneth Garrett/National Geographic Image Collection *page 1 (bottom)*. Getty *page 91 (right)*. Courtesy of NASA *pages 54 (inset), 55 (top left, bottom left & right), 56, 59, 61, 62, 63, 66, 69*. Taurins Design Associates *pages 1 (right), 2, 3 (top), 8, 13 (top)*.

Cover Design: Kristen Davis

Table of Contents

About the Math at Hand Problem-Solving Book

Most students struggle with math word problems. The *Math at Hand Problem-Solving Book* helps all students develop the reading, writing, and thinking skills they need to solve the word problems typically found in textbooks and on standardized tests. The step-by-step approach helps build student confidence in all four parts of the problem solving method—*Understand, Plan, Try,* and *Look Back*.

The *Math at Hand Problem-Solving Book* is an ideal companion to the *Math at Hand Handbook* or any math textbook.

Each chapter centers on a theme that is engaging, rich in math content, grade appropriate, and reading-level sensitive.

The problem-solving focus of each chapter is highlighted across the top—*Understand, Plan, Try,* and *Look Back*.

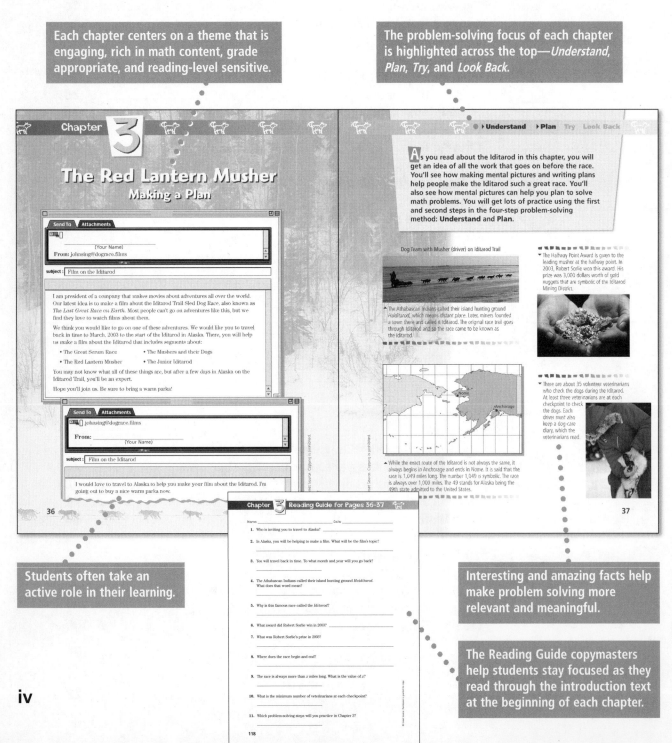

Students often take an active role in their learning.

Interesting and amazing facts help make problem solving more relevant and meaningful.

The Reading Guide copymasters help students stay focused as they read through the introduction text at the beginning of each chapter.

Research suggests that content-area reading comprehension is critical to student success in all disciplines and at all levels of competency.

The *Math at Hand Problem-Solving Book* adapts techniques used in remedial reading to teach students how to picture what is going on in a math word problem, to develop a plan, and then to solve and check their work. With the right tools to support their knowledge, students meet success as readers and problem solvers.

Charts, graphs, and other tools organize and display data. In the Problem-Solving Book, students learn how to look for, evaluate, and use all sorts of information. In the process they practice reasoning and critical-thinking skills.

Interdisciplinary topics explore math concepts in other subject areas and integrate real-world applications. Scaffolded instruction and graduated difficulty levels ensure thorough concept development.

Math at Hand references direct students to items in the handbook. Students can read more about a math topic, look up definitions, and so on.

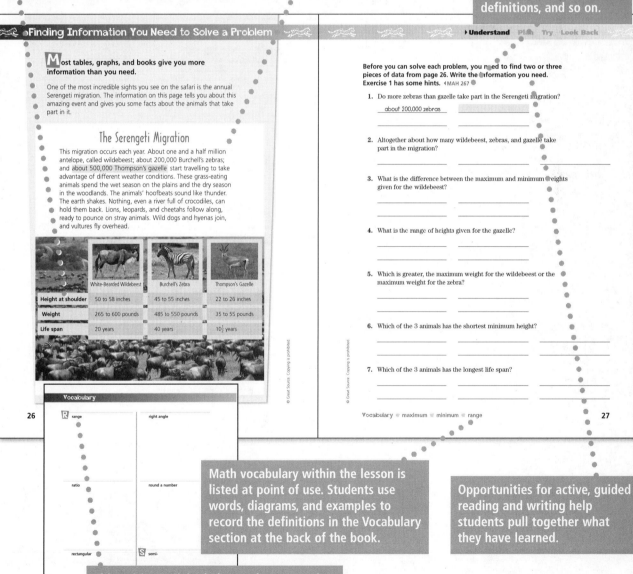

Finding Information You Need to Solve a Problem

▶Understand Plan Try Look Back

Most tables, graphs, and books give you more information than you need.

One of the most incredible sights you see on the safari is the annual Serengeti migration. The information on this page tells you about this amazing event and gives you some facts about the animals that take part in it.

The Serengeti Migration

This migration occurs each year. About one and a half million antelope, called wildebeest; about 200,000 Burchell's zebras; and about 500,000 Thompson's gazelle start travelling to take advantage of different weather conditions. These grass-eating animals spend the wet season on the plains and the dry season in the woodlands. The animals' hoofbeats sound like thunder. The earth shakes. Nothing, even a river full of crocodiles, can hold them back. Lions, leopards, and cheetahs follow along, ready to pounce on stray animals. Wild dogs and hyenas join, and vultures fly overhead.

	White-Bearded Wildebeest	Burchell's Zebra	Thompson's Gazelle
Height at shoulder	50 to 58 inches	45 to 55 inches	22 to 26 inches
Weight	265 to 600 pounds	485 to 550 pounds	35 to 55 pounds
Life span	20 years	40 years	$10\frac{1}{2}$ years

26

Before you can solve each problem, you need to find two or three pieces of data from page 26. Write the information you need. Exercise 1 has some hints. ◀MAH 267

1. Do more zebras than gazelle take part in the Serengeti migration?

   about 200,000 zebras _____

   _____ _____

2. Altogether about how many wildebeest, zebras, and gazelle take part in the migration?

   _____ _____

3. What is the difference between the maximum and minimum weights given for the wildebeest?

   _____ _____

   _____ _____

4. What is the range of heights given for the gazelle?

   _____ _____

   _____ _____

5. Which is greater, the maximum weight for the wildebeest or the maximum weight for the zebra?

   _____ _____

   _____ _____

6. Which of the 3 animals has the shortest minimum height?

   _____ _____ _____

7. Which of the 3 animals has the longest life span?

   _____ _____

   _____ _____

Vocabulary ● maximum ● minimum ● range

27

Vocabulary

R range	right angle
ratio	round a number
rectangular	**S** semi-

120

Math vocabulary within the lesson is listed at point of use. Students use words, diagrams, and examples to record the definitions in the Vocabulary section at the back of the book.

Opportunities for active, guided reading and writing help students pull together what they have learned.

This writing activity helps students organize, clarify, and refine their understanding of important math-related vocabulary.

v

The Teacher's Guide lessons are presented in an easy-to-use format.

Reduced student book lessons are supported with background notes, a teaching plan, and additional reference material at point of use.

Handbook items, at point of use, provide quick references for additional resources.

Active reading strategies help students identify, record, and define special math words. Once students understand the meaning of key vocabulary in each lesson, they have overcome major hurdles to success in solving math word problems.

The emphasis on reading and understanding is highlighted among the lesson objectives.

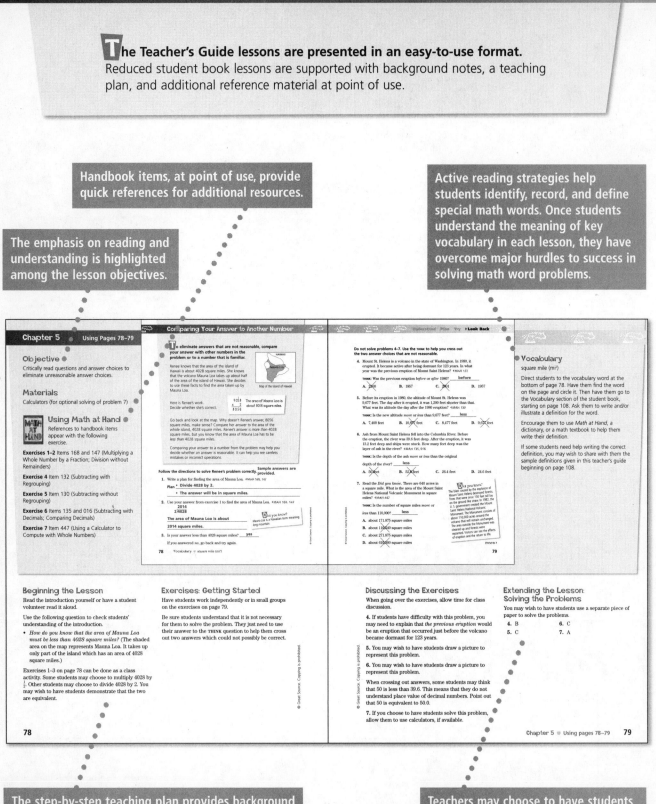

The step-by-step teaching plan provides background information and suggestions for assessing prior knowledge, getting started with the exercises, and encouraging discussion as students work through the exercises.

Teachers may choose to have students go beyond the lesson objectives and solve the problems. Where appropriate, answers to problems are provided.

Assessment

The *Math at Hand Problem-Solving Book* provides assessment in the form of chapter tests. Two forms of the chapter tests are available.

One form of the Chapter Test appears in the student book.

Answers for the student book chapter tests are printed in red in the teacher's guide.

Ideas for Struggling Learners are listed on the Assessment pages of the teacher's guide.

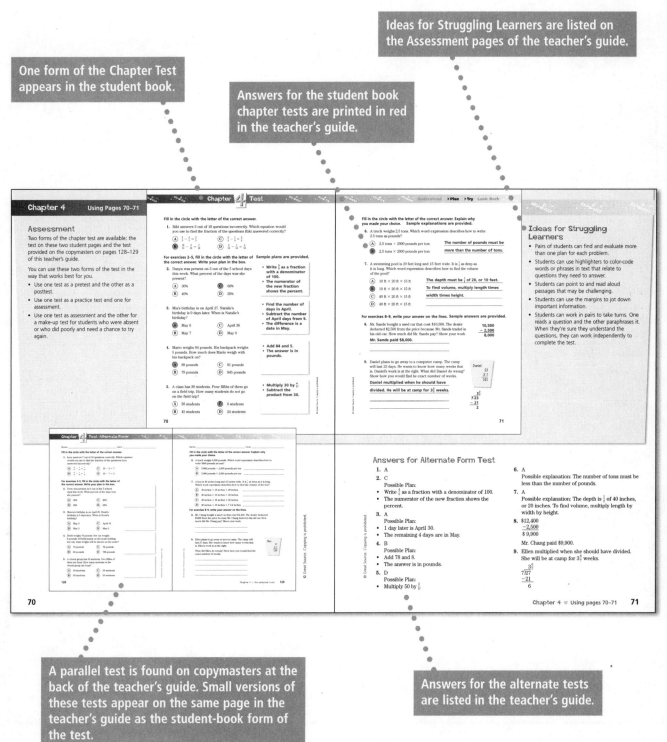

A parallel test is found on copymasters at the back of the teacher's guide. Small versions of these tests appear on the same page in the teacher's guide as the student-book form of the test.

Answers for the alternate tests are listed in the teacher's guide.

Problem-Solving Overview

The *Math at Hand Problem-Solving Book* focuses on reading and writing skills and the problem-solving method—*Understand, Plan, Try,* and *Look Back.* The table below identifies the pages on which some of the more specific problem-solving strategies and skills can be found.

Strategy or Skill	Chapter 1	Chapter 2	Chapter 3	Chapter 4	Chapter 5	Chapter 6
Solve in more than one way	14–15		46	59, 67		
Check for reasonableness					75–89	95, 97, 99, 101, 103–105, 107
Use an estimate or exact amount	8–9, 17			62	84–89	95, 97, 103–105, 107
Find needed information		30–33				94, 98, 105
Ignore unneeded information		22–23, 26–29, 34–35	47–48			94, 106
Use logical reasoning					75–89	101
Make or read a model	11–13, 17		39–40, 42–43, 52	58, 69–70		96
Make or read a diagram	10, 12		38, 40–41, 43, 52			94
Guess, check, and revise						96–101
Make or read a table		23, 26–27		66–67	82	
Make or read a graph		20–21, 23–25, 30, 32–35	50–51	65		
Use a simpler problem			42–44			
Write an equation or expression	17		39–43, 52	56–57. 70–71	84–87	
Write a plan			44–53	56–71	89	95–96, 98, 100, 103–106
Solve multi-step problems			44–53	56–71	89	96–97, 103–107
Combine strategies			42–43			96–107

Using the Math at Hand Handbook

Throughout the *Problem-Solving Book*, the lessons and exercises refer to the *Math at Hand handbook*, a math resource book for students. The item numbers identified in the lessons correspond with relevant topics in the handbook. Students can easily look up specific topics by item number for help with definitions, procedures, explanations, and rules. Teachers can use the handbooks to teach mini lessons on topics needing additional instruction.

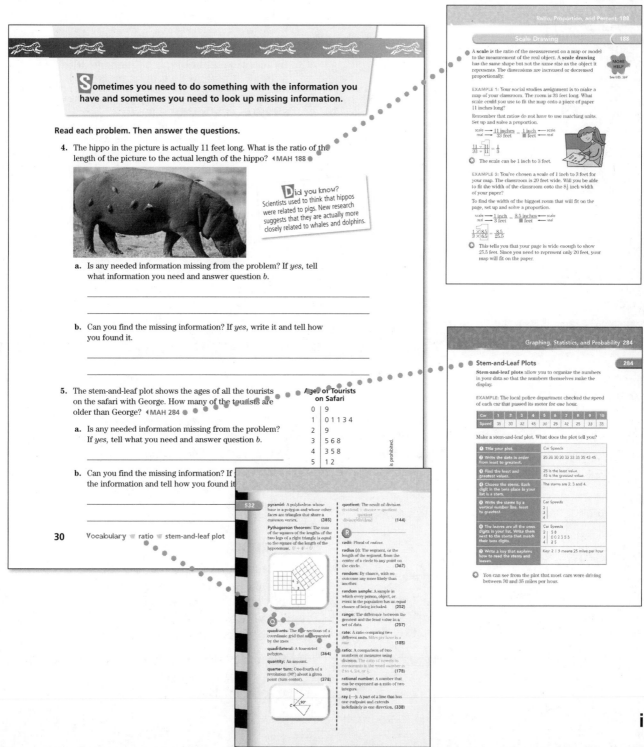

Sometimes you need to do something with the information you have and sometimes you need to look up missing information.

Read each problem. Then answer the questions.

4. The hippo in the picture is actually 11 feet long. What is the ratio of the length of the picture to the actual length of the hippo? ◀MAH 188

Did you know?
Scientists used to think that hippos were related to pigs. New research suggests that they are actually more closely related to whales and dolphins.

a. Is any needed information missing from the problem? If *yes*, tell what information you need and answer question *b*.

_____

_____

b. Can you find the missing information? If *yes*, write it and tell how you found it.

_____

_____

5. The stem-and-leaf plot shows the ages of all the tourists on the safari with George. How many of the tourists are older than George? ◀MAH 284

a. Is any needed information missing from the problem? If *yes*, tell what you need and answer question *b*.

_____

b. Can you find the missing information? If the information and tell how you found it

_____

_____

Ages of Tourists on Safari

0	9
1	0 1 1 3 4
2	9
3	5 6 8
4	3 5 8
5	1 2

30   Vocabulary ▪ ratio ▪ stem-and-leaf plot

The Wonders of Egypt

Reading Piece by Piece

Dear _____,
(Your Name)

Imagine you are in Egypt. You are at the tomb of one of the kings of ancient Egypt at the moment it is opened. You see a mummy, a body that is thousands of years old and was wrapped in cloth, surrounded by jewels and gold statues. This would be a very exciting day for an archaeologist on a dig in Egypt.

Would you like to join me on a dig to discover the secrets of ancient Egypt? I'm inviting you because you are learning to solve math problems and we need people who can solve problems. For example, we have discovered that many of the people who died at a young age in ancient Egypt had damaged backs. We think that workers in Egypt long ago carried very heavy things and this is why their skeletons show signs of stress, but we're still working on the problem.

We sift through mud, all kinds of debris, and animal bones to try to figure out what life was like thousands of years ago. We are very lucky that the climate is so dry in Egypt. This means that many things are preserved—they have not rotted away because of dampness.

There are all kinds of ways that we dig. We use robots to go through shafts and explore areas that we can't reach. We've even gone underwater to explore Queen Cleopatra's palace.

Sound exciting? I hope you think so and that you'll join me on an incredible adventure into the past. Before you go, you'll need to learn as much about Egypt as you can.

Sincerely,

Janet Lu, Ph.D.

Using Page 1

Guiding the Reading

Have students write their own names in the space provided in the letter. Then ask them to read these two pages independently. Use the copymaster on page 116 of this book to help guide their reading.

Explain the meaning of the word *dig*, a search conducted by archaeologists through ancient ruins.

Connecting to the Theme

These are optional ideas for connecting to the theme of Egypt as you do this chapter.

- Divide your students into small groups. Have each group research and give a report on a different pyramid. A good source of information is the National Geographic site listed on page 1.

- Have students look at the Time Warp Gallery website to see artist Richard Deurer's paintings with images of ancient Egypt and modern times. Have student create their own paintings that incorporate both ancient and modern images. You might even want to have the whole class work together to create a mural.

Bibliography

Logan, Claudia. *The 5,000-Year-Old Puzzle.* New York: Farrar, Straus, and Giroux, 2002.
A book about the mystery surrounding an Egyptian tomb that was discovered in 1924. It is based on the actual records of an archaeological dig.

Shuter, Jane. *Egypt (part of the Ancient World series).* Austin, TX: Steck-Vaughn, 1999.
A book about ancient Egypt.

In this chapter, you will learn about Egypt and then take a trip there to participate in an archaeological dig. You'll need to be sure you read carefully so that the information you collect is correct. You'll need to pay special attention to words, phrases, sentences, and symbols. You'll get plenty of practice using the first step of the four-step problem-solving method: **Understand.**

◀ Archaeologists sift through mud and dirt to find objects from ancient Egypt. These objects tell a story about life in ancient Egypt.

▼ Archaeologists know from the art in the tombs that these pots were used to bake bread.

▲ Ancient Egyptians believed that their king ruled even after his death. Kings' tombs were more important than their palaces. The resting place after death was an immense structure called a pyramid. This pyramid, at Sakkara, is the oldest in Egypt.

1

Websites

The Time Warp Gallery
http://members.aol.com/egyptwarp/warp.html
   Artist Richard Deurer does paintings that incorporate images from both ancient Egypt and modern life.

National Geographic: Secrets of Egypt
http://www.nationalgeographic.com/pyramids/
   Explore different pyramids; read the journal of Nancy Gupton, who took a 4-day expedition to ancient Egyptian sites; learn how to make a mummy.

Sample Answers for Reading Guide

1. Egypt
2. Janet Lu, Ph.D.
3. Many skeletons with damaged backs have been found.
4. The climate in Egypt is dry.
5. archaeologists
6. Art in tombs shows similar pots being used for baking bread.
7. his tomb
8. a pyramid
9. Understand, Plan, Try, Look Back
10. Understand

Chapter 1 **Reading Guide for Page 1**

Name _____ Date _____

1. In this chapter, you're taking an imaginary trip to what country?
   _____

2. Who is inviting you to go to this country? _____

3. Why do we suspect that workers from ancient Egypt carried very heavy things?
   _____

4. Why are so many things from ancient Egypt well-preserved and not rotted away?
   _____

5. What name is given to people who study ancient civilizations by searching through ancient ruins?
   _____

6. Look at the pots shown on page 1. How do we know these pots were used for baking bread?
   _____

7. What was more important than a palace to an ancient Egyptian king?
   _____

8. What structure was used as a tomb for an ancient Egyptian king?
   _____

9. What are the steps in the four-step problem-solving method?
   _____

10. Which problem-solving step will you practice in Chapter 1?
   _____

116

Objectives

Read for understanding.

Paraphrase.

Understand common math terms.

Find math words that have different meanings in everyday life.

Using Math at Hand

References to handbook items appear with the following exercises.

Exercise 1 Items 237–239 (Expressions)

Exercise 2 Items 063 and 500 (Even and Odd Numbers; Egyptian Numerals)

Exercise 3 Item 369 (Similarity)

Exercise 4 Items 106 and 100 (Estimating Products, Sums, and Differences); 382 (Solid Figures); 337 (Lines); 299 (Area); 260 (Mean)

Optional Follow Up

Ask students to think of other words for which the everyday meaning is different from the math meaning. On the chalkboard, make a list of the words students suggest. (Possible answers: positive, negative, leg, flip, slide, turn, compatible, net)

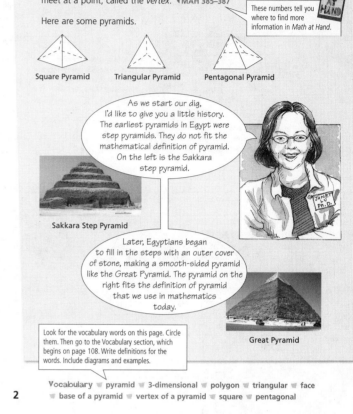

Sometimes the same word can mean different things.

Sometimes the math meaning of a word isn't exactly the same as the everyday meaning of the word. You can get an idea about the meaning of a word by looking at how it is used.

In math, the word *pyramid* is used to describe some 3-dimensional figures. The figure must have exactly one base that is a polygon. It has one triangular face for each side of the base. The triangular faces all meet at a point, called the *vertex*. ◄ MAH 385–387

These numbers tell you where to find more information in *Math at Hand*.

Here are some pyramids.

Square Pyramid   Triangular Pyramid   Pentagonal Pyramid

As we start our dig, I'd like to give you a little history. The earliest pyramids in Egypt were step pyramids. They do not fit the mathematical definition of pyramid. On the left is the Sakkara step pyramid.

Sakkara Step Pyramid

Later, Egyptians began to fill in the steps with an outer cover of stone, making a smooth-sided pyramid like the Great Pyramid. The pyramid on the right fits the definition of pyramid that we use in mathematics today.

Great Pyramid

Look for the vocabulary words on this page. Circle them. Then go to the Vocabulary section, which begins on page 108. Write definitions for the words. Include diagrams and examples.

Vocabulary ▾ pyramid ▾ 3-dimensional ▾ polygon ▾ triangular ▾ face ▾ base of a pyramid ▾ vertex of a pyramid ▾ square ▾ pentagonal

2

Beginning the Lesson

Read the introduction yourself or ask a volunteer to read it aloud.

Use these questions to check students' understanding of the introduction.

- *Is a triangle a pyramid? Why or why not?* (No. A triangle is not a 3-dimensional figure.)

- *How can you describe the base of any pyramid?* (It is always a polygon.)

Exercises: Getting Started

Have students work independently or in small groups on the exercises on page 3. Explain that for exercises 1–3, students will need to choose the same word to use in both sentences. For exercise 4, they will need to choose one word from the box and write two sentences, one that shows the everyday meaning of the word and one that shows the math meaning.

For exercises 1–3, use the same word to complete each of the two sentences.

1. a. King Tut is famous because, when his tomb was discovered, it was in very good condition. Most other tombs had been robbed. In this picture, King Tut has a serious _____**expression**_____ on his face.

   b. The value of the _____**expression**_____ 20 + 30 is 50. ◂MAH 237–239

2. a. You may find it _____**odd**_____ that King Tut was married at the age of 8 and became king of Egypt when he was 9.

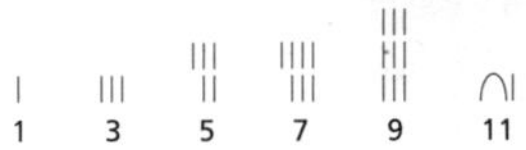

	||| || |||| ||| ∩
1	3	5	7	9	11

   b. The picture shows how Egyptians wrote the _____**odd**_____ numbers 1 through 11. ◂MAH 063, 500

3. a. Cats were very important to the Egyptians. The cat most like those owned by ancient Egyptians is the Egyptian Mau. The two copies of a photograph show what an Egyptian Mau looks like. They are the same shape but not the same size, so they are _____**similar**_____. ◂MAH 369

   b. Houses in ancient Egypt looked _____**similar**_____ because they were all made of mud bricks and had flat roofs.

4. Choose one word from the box. Write one sentence that shows an everyday meaning and one sentence that shows the math meaning.
   Sample answers are provided.

   a. _____
      Rice is an important product of China.

   b. _____
      The product of 3 and 6 is 18.
      _____
      _____

product ◂MAH 106
difference ◂MAH 100
face ◂MAH 382
line ◂MAH 337
area ◂MAH 299
mean ◂MAH 260
more ▸

Vocabulary ▼ product ▼ difference ▼ line ▼ area ▼ mean   **3**

Vocabulary

area	polygon
base of a pyramid	product
difference	pyramid
face	square
line	3-dimensional
mean	triangular
pentagonal	vertex of a pyramid

Direct students to the vocabulary words at the bottom of each page. Have them find each word on the page and circle it. Then have them go to the Vocabulary section of the student book, starting on page 108. Ask them to write and/or illustrate a definition for the words.

Encourage students to use *Math at Hand*, a dictionary, or a math textbook to help them write their definitions.

If some students need help writing correct definitions, you may wish to share with them the sample definitions given in this teacher's guide starting on page 108.

Discussing the Exercises

When going over the exercises, allow time for class discussion.

1–3. If no students are able to name the same word that fits in both sentences, direct them to use the handbook, *Math at Hand*. Item numbers appear in the student book.

4. Have volunteers read their sentences aloud. Try to choose students so that sentences for all word-choices are read. If there is a word that no one chose, have volunteers think of sentences that show the two meanings. If students are not familiar with the mathematical meaning of the word, they can check in the handbook.

Objective

Understand that some math words have multiple meanings.

Using Math at Hand

References to handbook items appear with the following exercises.

Exercise 5 Items 365 (Classifying Quadrilaterals); 382 and 385 (Solid Figures); 299 (Area); 067 (Squares and Square Roots)

Exercise 6 Items 028 and 029 (Fractions); 529 (Glossary entry: Ordinal Numbers)

Exercise 7 Items 057 (Common Factors); 061 (Least Common Multiple); 519 (Glossary entry: common)

Exercise 8 Items 320 and 347 (Fahrenheit; Naming Different-Size Angles)

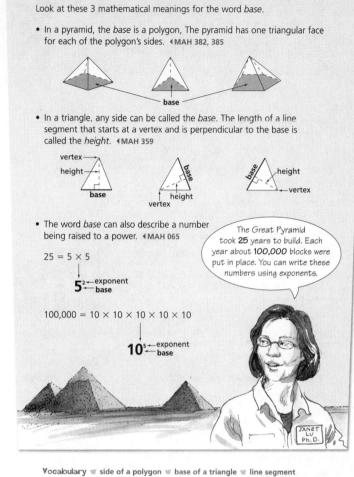

Beginning the Lesson

Read the introduction yourself or ask a volunteer to read it aloud.

Use the following questions to check students' understanding of the introduction.

- *What word is used in three different ways on page 4?* (base)
- *In a pyramid, how do you know which face is the base?* (The base of each triangular face makes one side of the base of the pyramid.)
- *In a triangle, how do you know which side is the base?* (Any side can be a base.)

Exercises: Getting Started

Have students work independently or in small groups on the exercises on page 5. Explain that they will need to choose the same word to use for all of the sentences in each exercise.

4

Each exercise contains a group of sentences. Use the same word to complete each of the sentences in the group.

5. a. The base of the Great Pyramid is a _____ square _____. ◀MAH 365, 382, 385

 b. Egypt covers an area of 386,650 _____ square _____ miles, which is about the same as the area of Texas and California together. ◀MAH 299

 c. The _____ square _____ of 3 is 9. ◀MAH 067

6. a. In ancient Egypt, when a man and woman married, they combined their property. The man would provide two thirds and the woman would provide the remaining _____ third _____. ◀MAH 028–029

 b. During his _____ third _____ year as ruler, King Tut lived in the City of the Disc, a city named for the sun. ◀MAH 529

 c. The trip to Egypt will begin on October 3, or the _____ third _____ day of October. ◀MAH 529

7. a. The _____ common _____ factors of 6 and 16 are 1 and 2. ◀MAH 057

 b. Six is a _____ common _____ multiple of 2 and 3. ◀MAH 061

 c. The numerator and denominator of a _____ common _____ fraction are whole numbers. ◀MAH 519

8. a. Two temperature scales are _____ degrees _____ Fahrenheit and _____ degrees _____ Celsius.

 b. In Cairo, Egypt, the average high temperature in August is 92 _____ degrees _____ Fahrenheit. ◀MAH 320

 c. The measure of this angle is 90 _____ degrees _____. right angle ◀MAH 347

more ▶

Vocabulary ▾ numerator ▾ denominator ▾ fraction ▾ factor ▾ multiple ▾ average ▾ Fahrenheit ▾ right angle ▾ Celsius

5

Vocabulary

average	height of a triangle
base in exponential notation	line segment
base of a triangle	multiple
Celsius	numerator
denominator	perpendicular
factor	power
Fahrenheit	right angle
fraction	side of a polygon

Direct students to the vocabulary words at the bottom of each page. Have them find each word on the page and circle it. Then have them go to the Vocabulary section of the student book, starting on page 108. Ask them to write and/or illustrate definitions for the words.

Encourage students to use *Math at Hand*, a dictionary, or a math textbook to help them write their definitions.

If some students need help writing correct definitions, you may wish to share with them the sample definitions given in this teacher's guide starting on page 108.

Discussing the Exercises

When going over the exercises, allow time for class discussion.

5–8. If no students are able to name the same word that fits in all of the sentences in the group, direct them to use *Math at Hand*. Item numbers appear in the student book.

Objectives

Use synonyms.

Paraphrase.

Using Math at Hand

References to handbook items appear with the following exercises.

Exercise 11 Item 317 (Weight)

Exercise 13 Items 004–005 (Reading and Writing Whole Numbers)

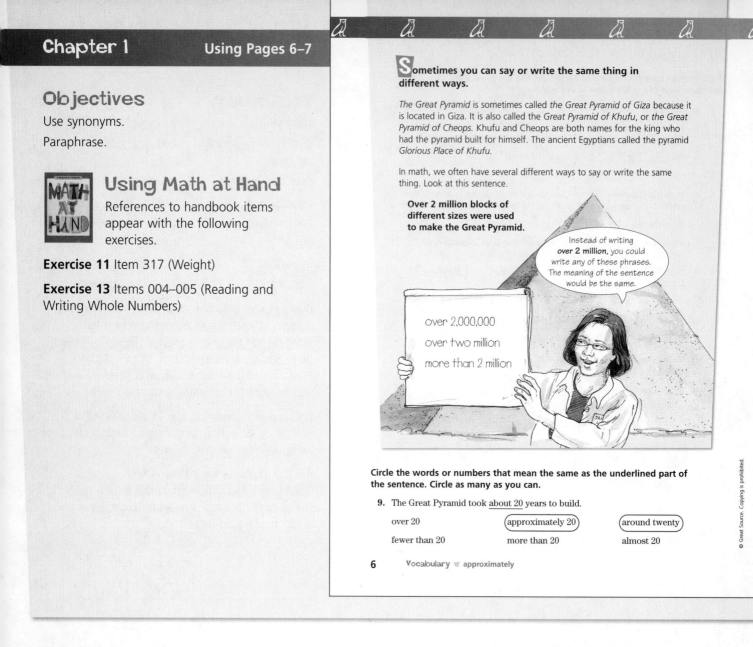

Sometimes you can say or write the same thing in different ways.

The Great Pyramid is sometimes called *the Great Pyramid of Giza* because it is located in Giza. It is also called the *Great Pyramid of Khufu*, or *the Great Pyramid of Cheops*. Khufu and Cheops are both names for the king who had the pyramid built for himself. The ancient Egyptians called the pyramid *Glorious Place of Khufu*.

In math, we often have several different ways to say or write the same thing. Look at this sentence.

Over 2 million blocks of different sizes were used to make the Great Pyramid.

Instead of writing **over 2 million**, you could write any of these phrases. The meaning of the sentence would be the same.

over 2,000,000

over two million

more than 2 million

Circle the words or numbers that mean the same as the underlined part of the sentence. Circle as many as you can.

9. The Great Pyramid took about 20 years to build.

    over 20   (approximately 20)   (around twenty)

    fewer than 20   more than 20   almost 20

6   Vocabulary ⬥ approximately

Beginning the Lesson

Read the introduction yourself or ask a volunteer to read it aloud.

Use the following questions to check students' understanding of the introduction.

- *What other names for the Great Pyramid are mentioned on page 6?* (The Great Pyramid of Giza, the Great Pyramid of Khufu, the Great Pyramid of Cheops, Glorious Place of Khufu)

- *Can you think of any other ways to write* over 2 million? (Possible answer; More than 2,000,000)

Exercises: Getting Started

Have students work independently or in small groups on the exercises on pages 6–7. Some students may find it helpful to cross out wrong answers.

10. The Great Pyramid was built more than 4,000 years ago.

at most 4000 years   4000 or more years

fewer than 4000 years   over 4 centuries   (over 4000 years)

11. Each perfectly-cut stone block in the Great Pyramid weighed at least $2\frac{1}{2}$ tons. ◀MAH 317

less than 2.5 tons   (2.5 tons or more)   at least 2100 pounds

(5000 pounds or more)   less than 2.5 pounds

12. The Great Pyramid covered a dozen or more acres.

less than 13 acres   (no less than 12 acres)   (at least 12 acres)

13. Each summer the flooding of the Nile River gave Egyptians fertile soil. The Nile River, 4240 miles long, is the longest river in the world. ◀MAH 004, 005

four hundred twenty-four   four thousand, twenty-four

over 4 million   less than 4000   (four thousand, two hundred forty)

14. Ancient Egypt had a barter economy. This means that the economy was based on trading, not money. For example, one pair of sandals was worth 2 to 4 pounds of copper.

more than 4   (at least 2 but not more than 4)

less than 2   (about 3)

one half   1 to 2

Did you know?
In ancient Egypt, most people went barefoot, especially women and children. Sometimes, however, sandals were worn at important events. The toes of the sandals were curled up to keep out the sand.

more ▶

© Great Source. Copying is prohibited.

Vocabulary

approximately	mile (mi)
century	pound (lb)
dozen	ton (t)

Direct students to the vocabulary words at the bottom of each page. Have them find each word on the page and circle it. Then have them go to the Vocabulary section of the student book, starting on page 108. Ask them to write and/or illustrate a definition for the words.

Encourage students to use *Math at Hand*, a dictionary, or a math textbook to help them write their definitions.

If some students need help writing correct definitions, you may wish to share with them the sample definitions given in this teacher's guide starting on page 108.

Discussing the Exercises

When going over the exercises, allow time for class discussion.

9. *Why is* fewer than 20 *not correct?* (Possible answer: 21 is about 20, but it is not fewer than 20.)

10. *How many years are in a century?* (100 years) *Why is* 4,000 or more years *not correct?* (More than 4,000 can't be exactly 4,000.)

11. *How many pounds are in a ton?* (2,000) *In* $1\frac{1}{2}$ *tons?* (5,000)

12. *When we say* a dozen or more, *can the number be 12?* (yes) *13?* (yes) *11?* (no)

13. *Is there another way to say 4240?* (Possible answer: forty-two hundred forty) *How do you write* four hundred twenty-four? (424) *How do you write four thousand, twenty-four?"* (4,024)

© Great Source. Copying is prohibited.

Objectives

Read actively.

Understand the different forms numbers can take.

Understand the difference between exact numbers and estimates.

Using Math at Hand

References to handbook items appear with the following exercises.

Exercises 15–19 Item 414 (Choose an Estimate or Exact Amount)

Connecting to the Theme

The *Did You Know?* on this page gives the web address for a currency converter. For several days, have students look up the value of a U. S. dollar in Egyptian pounds and make a line graph of the results. Students will see that the values are not constant; they can vary from day to day.

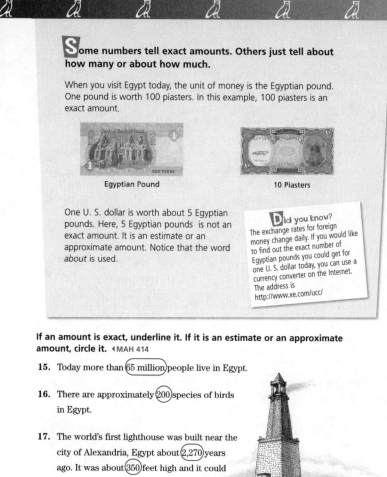

Some numbers tell exact amounts. Others just tell about how many or about how much.

When you visit Egypt today, the unit of money is the Egyptian pound. One pound is worth 100 piasters. In this example, 100 piasters is an exact amount.

Egyptian Pound

10 Piasters

One U. S. dollar is worth about 5 Egyptian pounds. Here, 5 Egyptian pounds is not an exact amount. It is an estimate or an approximate amount. Notice that the word *about* is used.

Did you know?
The exchange rates for foreign money change daily. If you would like to find out the exact number of Egyptian pounds you could get for one U. S. dollar today, you can use a currency converter on the Internet. The address is http://www.xe.com/ucc/

If an amount is exact, underline it. If it is an estimate or an approximate amount, circle it. ◄MAH 414

15. Today more than (65 million) people live in Egypt.

16. There are approximately (200) species of birds in Egypt.

17. The world's first lighthouse was built near the city of Alexandria, Egypt about (2,270) years ago. It was about (350) feet high and it could be seen from more than (30) miles out at sea.

8   Vocabulary ▼ estimate (*noun*)

Beginning the Lesson

Read the introduction yourself or ask a volunteer to read it aloud.

Use the following question to check students' understanding of the introduction.

• *How can you be sure 5 is an estimate?* (The word *about* is used with it.)

Exercises: Getting Started

Have students work independently or in small groups on the exercises on pages 8–9.

18. Egypt is located in the northwest corner of Africa. It is the <u>twelfth</u> largest country in Africa.

The Nile River is about (4240) miles long and is the longest river in the world. About (1000) miles of it run through Egypt. In ancient times, the river would flood each summer and give Egyptians fertile soil. In modern times, a dam has changed this pattern and the last flood occurred around (1960.)

EGYPT

19. In <u>1922</u>, the discovery of King Tut's tomb made headlines all over the world. (Two) years or so later, Dr. George Reisner and a team of archaeologists explored a site near the Great Pyramid. There they discovered the tomb of Queen Hetep-heres, the mother of King Khufu. Many treasures were found. In addition to a chest containing the remains of the queen, there were <u>30</u> alabaster containers, a jewelry box containing <u>20</u> silver bracelets, and the queen's bed.

The exploration of this site, known as Giza <u>7000X</u>, took <u>321</u> working days. <u>One thousand fifty-seven</u> photographs were taken as well as more than (1700) pages of notes and drawings. Every move of the dig was recorded exactly.

If you would like to learn more about this famous archaeological dig, read the book *The (5,000) Year-Old Puzzle* by Claudia Logan. The book is <u>48</u> pages long and has many interesting pictures. It will give you a good idea about what an archaeological dig is like.

9

Vocabulary

estimate (*noun*)

Direct students to the vocabulary word at the bottom of page 8. Have them find the word on the page and circle it. Then have them go to the Vocabulary section of the student book, starting on page 108. Ask them to write and/or illustrate a definition for the word.

Encourage students to use *Math at Hand*, a dictionary, or a math textbook to help them write their definition.

If some students need help writing the correct definition, you may wish to share with them the sample definition given in this teacher's guide starting on page 108.

Optional Follow Up

Have students find examples of exact and estimated numbers in newspapers and magazines. Make a bulletin board display. Place exact numbers on one side and estimated numbers on the other side.

Discussing the Exercises

When going over the exercises, allow time for class discussion. Sometimes it's hard to tell whether a number is an estimate or an exact amount. For example, a 400-page book could be a reference to a book exactly 400 pages long, but probably isn't. When you write, you can be clearer by using qualifiers like *exactly*, *about*, *approximately*, etc. Have students look for these qualifiers to help them decide which words are estimates.

19. Students may disagree about whether the number 5,000 is exact or an estimate. Accept either answer if the student can support that answer. While 5,000 is exactly the number given in the title of the book, it is an approximate or rounded number that refers to the age of ancient Egypt.

Objectives

Visualize a situation.

Choose a picture to describe a situation.

Using Math at Hand

References to handbook items appear with the following exercises.

Exercise 1 Items 004 and 136 (Whole Numbers: Place Value; Multiplication)

Exercise 2 Item 033 (Fraction of a Set)

Exercise 3 Item 365 (Classifying Quadrilaterals)

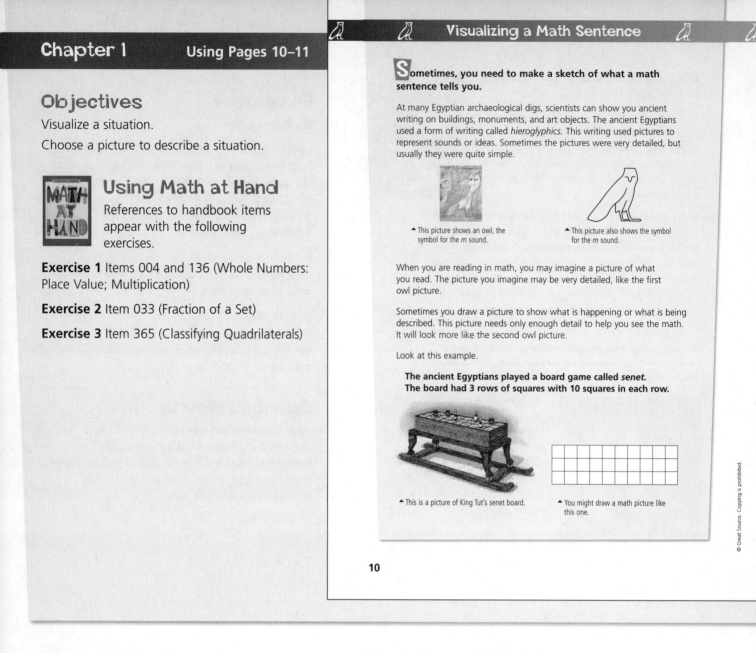

Sometimes, you need to make a sketch of what a math sentence tells you.

At many Egyptian archaeological digs, scientists can show you ancient writing on buildings, monuments, and art objects. The ancient Egyptians used a form of writing called *hieroglyphics*. This writing used pictures to represent sounds or ideas. Sometimes the pictures were very detailed, but usually they were quite simple.

▲ This picture shows an owl, the symbol for the *m* sound.

▲ This picture also shows the symbol for the *m* sound.

When you are reading in math, you may imagine a picture of what you read. The picture you imagine may be very detailed, like the first owl picture.

Sometimes you draw a picture to show what is happening or what is being described. This picture needs only enough detail to help you see the math. It will look more like the second owl picture.

Look at this example.

The ancient Egyptians played a board game called *senet*. The board had 3 rows of squares with 10 squares in each row.

▲ This is a picture of King Tut's senet board.

▲ You might draw a math picture like this one.

10

Beginning the Lesson

Write the word *hieroglyphics* on the board and model how to pronounce it: hy-roh-GLIHF-ihks. Then read the introduction yourself or ask a volunteer to read it aloud.

Use the following question to check students' understanding of the introduction.

- *When drawing a picture in math, what do you think is most important to show?* (Possible answer: Show how the numbers are related.)

Exercises: Getting Started

Have students work independently or in small groups on the exercises on page 11.

In front of exercises 1–3, write the letter of the picture that best shows the meaning of the math.

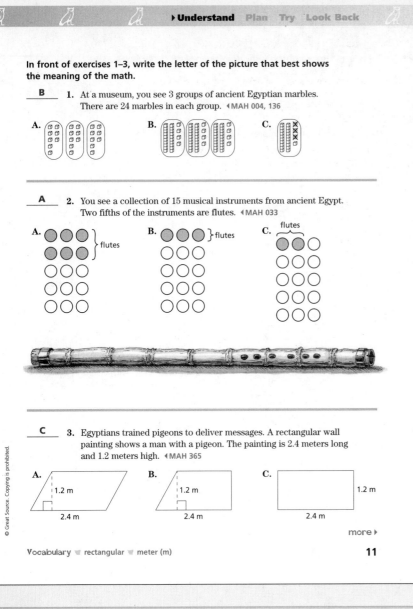

____B____   **1.** At a museum, you see 3 groups of ancient Egyptian marbles. There are 24 marbles in each group. ◂MAH 004, 136

A.   **B.**   **C.**

____A____   **2.** You see a collection of 15 musical instruments from ancient Egypt. Two fifths of the instruments are flutes. ◂MAH 033

A. }flutes   **B.** }flutes   **C.** flutes

____C____   **3.** Egyptians trained pigeons to deliver messages. A rectangular wall painting shows a man with a pigeon. The painting is 2.4 meters long and 1.2 meters high. ◂MAH 365

A. 1.2 m 2.4 m   **B.** 1.2 m 2.4 m   **C.** 1.2 m 2.4 m

more ▸

Vocabulary ▾ rectangular ▾ meter (m)

11

Vocabulary

rectangular

meter (m)

Direct students to the vocabulary words at the bottom of page 11. Have them find each word on the page and circle it. Then have them go to the Vocabulary section of the student book, starting on page 108. Ask them to write and/or illustrate definitions for the words.

Encourage students to use *Math at Hand*, a dictionary, or a math textbook to help them write their definitions.

If some students need help writing correct definitions, you may wish to share with them the sample definitions given in this teacher's guide starting on page 108.

Discussing the Exercises

When going over the exercises, allow time for class discussion.

1. *Look at picture B (the correct picture). What does each loop stand for?* (a group) *What does each block stand for?* (a marble) *Look at picture A. What could this picture represent?* (Possible answer: 3 equal groups of marbles; 24 marbles in all) *Look at picture C. What could this picture represent?* (Possible answer: 24 marbles, 3 taken away)

2. *Look at picture A (the correct picture). What does it show?* ($\frac{2}{5}$ of 15) *Look at picture B. What does it show?* ($\frac{1}{5}$ of 15) *Look at picture C. What does it show?* (2 out of 15)

3. *Look at picture C (the correct picture). What shape is shown?* (a rectangle)

Objectives

Visualize a mathematical situation.

Sketch a mathematical situation.

Using Math at Hand

References to handbook items appear with the following exercises.

Exercise 4 Item 033 (Fraction of a Set)

Exercise 6 Items 309 and 310 (Volume of Prisms)

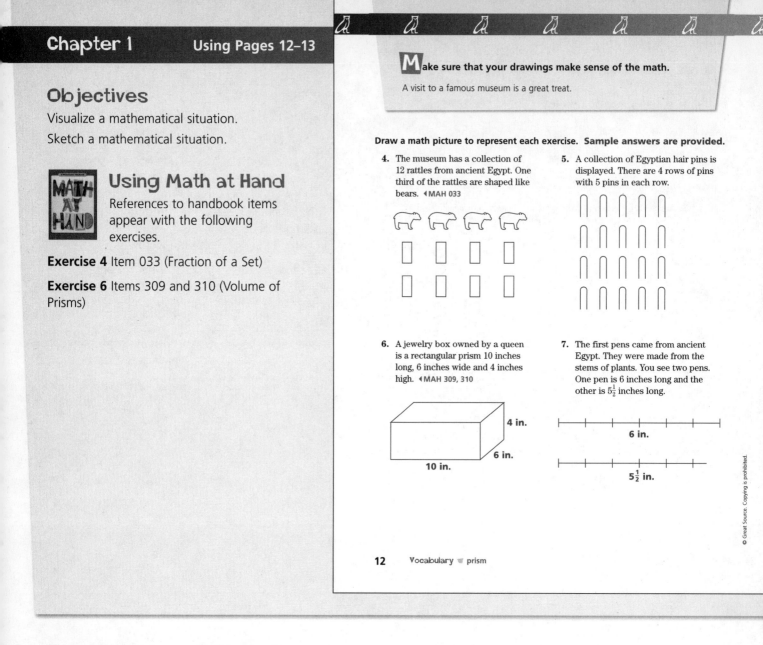

Make sure that your drawings make sense of the math.

A visit to a famous museum is a great treat.

Draw a math picture to represent each exercise. Sample answers are provided.

4. The museum has a collection of 12 rattles from ancient Egypt. One third of the rattles are shaped like bears. ◀ MAH 033

5. A collection of Egyptian hair pins is displayed. There are 4 rows of pins with 5 pins in each row.

6. A jewelry box owned by a queen is a rectangular prism 10 inches long, 6 inches wide and 4 inches high. ◀ MAH 309, 310

4 in.

6 in.

10 in.

7. The first pens came from ancient Egypt. They were made from the stems of plants. You see two pens. One pen is 6 inches long and the other is $5\frac{1}{2}$ inches long.

6 in.

$5\frac{1}{2}$ in.

12   Vocabulary ▼ prism

Exercises: Getting Started

Have students work independently or in small groups on the exercises on pages 12–13. Remind students that they should draw a picture that shows the math. The picture should not be very detailed.

Cross out the picture that does *not* show the math in the sentence.

8. One hundred nine children and fourteen adults will go on the trip to Egypt. ◄ MAH 004

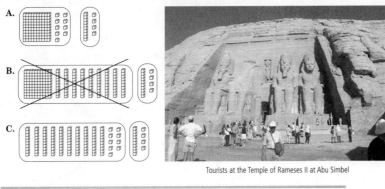

Tourists at the Temple of Rameses II at Abu Simbel

9. Seventy-five percent of your class will go on the trip. ◄ MAH 190, 044

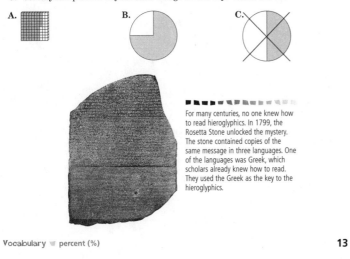

For many centuries, no one knew how to read hieroglyphics. In 1799, the Rosetta Stone unlocked the mystery. The stone contained copies of the same message in three languages. One of the languages was Greek, which scholars already knew how to read. They used the Greek as the key to the hieroglyphics.

Vocabulary ◼ percent (%)

13

Vocabulary

percent (%)

prism

Direct students to the vocabulary words at the bottom of each page. Have them find the words on the pages and circle them. Then have them go to the Vocabulary section of the student book, starting on page 108. Ask them to write and/or illustrate a definition for each word.

Encourage students to use *Math at Hand*, a dictionary, or a math textbook to help them write their definition.

If some students need help writing correct definition, you may wish to share with them the sample definition given in this teacher's guide starting on page 108.

Discussing the Exercises

When going over the exercises, allow time for class discussion.

4–7. Have volunteers draw their pictures on the board. If some students drew different pictures, have them share and explain their work. Emphasize that there can be more than one correct picture.

Objectives

Reason logically.

Interpret mathematical symbols.

Translate everyday language into mathematical language.

Using Math at Hand

References to handbook items appear with the following exercises.

Exercises 1–4 Items 008 and 514 (Comparing Whole Numbers; Glossary of Mathematical Symbols)

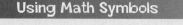
A symbol represents a word or group of words.

You have learned how ancient Egyptian writing was based on symbols that represented ideas and sounds. Egyptians used symbols for numbers, too. Here is the symbol they used for one million.

Some people think this symbol shows a man throwing up his hands, as if to say, I can't count any higher!

1,000,000

In our mathematical system, we often use symbols for numbers but we also use symbols as a short way to write a word or phrase.

Write one of the symbols from below in each ◯ so that the 2 sentences in each pair give the same information. ◀MAH 008, 514

$$+ \quad - \quad \times \quad \div \quad > \quad < \quad =$$

1. On Monday, you found more than 3 items.

    a. The number of items you found on Monday ⟨ > ⟩ 3.

    b. 3 ⟨ < ⟩ the number of items you found on Monday.

14

Beginning the Lesson

Read the introduction yourself or ask a volunteer to read it aloud.

Exercises: Getting Started

Have students work independently or in small groups on the exercises on pages 14–15. Review the meaning of > (is greater than) and < (is less than). Remind them that the symbol always points to the number with less value.

Point out that students are to write a symbol in each oval and that there may be more than one possible pair of symbols for some sentences. Some students may use the greater than and less than symbols in some exercises to create different sentences than the samples we've shown. Give credit whenever both sentences in each group give the same information.

2. On Tuesday, you and your partner found 7 items altogether.

    a. The number of items you found on Tuesday $\boxed{+}$ the number of items your partner found on Tuesday $\boxed{=}$ 7.

    b. 7 $\boxed{=}$ the number of items you found on Tuesday $\boxed{+}$ the number of items your partner found on Tuesday.

                        (or, 7 $\boxed{-}$ the number you. . . $\boxed{=}$)

3. The total number of coins found is twice the total number of statue pieces found.

    a. The total number of coins found $\boxed{÷}$ 2 $\boxed{=}$ the total number of statue pieces found.

                          (or. . . found $\boxed{=}$ 2 $\boxed{×}$ . . .)

    b. The total number of statue pieces found $\boxed{×}$ 2 $\boxed{=}$ the total number of coins found.

4. The total number of gold pieces found is 4 less than the total number of jewels found.

    a. The total number of gold pieces found $\boxed{=}$ the total number of jewels found $\boxed{-}$ 4.

    b. The total number of jewels found $\boxed{-}$ the total number of gold pieces found $\boxed{=}$ 4.

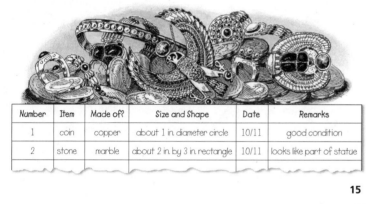

Number	Item	Made of?	Size and Shape	Date	Remarks
1	coin	copper	about 1 in. diameter circle	10/11	good condition
2	stone	marble	about 2 in. by 3 in. rectangle	10/11	looks like part of statue

15

Discussing the Exercises

When going over the exercises, allow time for class discussion.

2b. There are at least two possible answers here:
= and + or – and =.
Encourage students to find both answers.

3a. There are at least two possible answers here:
÷ and = or = and ×.
Encourage students to find both answers.

Assessment

Two forms of the chapter test are available: the test on these two student pages and the test provided on the copymasters on pages 122–123 of this teacher's guide.

You can use these two forms of the test in the way that works best for you.

- Use one test as a pretest and the other as a posttest.
- Use one test as a practice test and one for assessment.
- Use one test as assessment and the other for a make-up test for students who were absent or who did poorly and need a chance to try again.

Fill in the circle with the letter of the correct answer.

1. Which of these figures does *not* show a pyramid?

   (A)   (B)   (C)   (D)

2. Which of the following is an odd number?

   (A) 6   (B) 10   (C) 17   (D) 4

3. Nick's age in exponential notation is 4^2. In this number, what is the base?

   (A) 4   (B) 2   (C) 16   (D) 8

For exercises 4–6, mark the letter of the group of words that means the same as the underlined words.

4. Mrs. Griggs bought 2.5 pounds of cheese.

   (A) 25 pounds   (C) two and one half pounds
   (B) two and one fifth pounds   (D) 2.5 tons

5. The American Revolution took place over 200 years ago.

   (A) less than 2 centuries   (C) less than 200 years
   (B) more than 2 centuries   (D) almost 200 years

6. There were at least 12 people at the play.

   (A) 12 or less   (C) less than 12
   (B) exactly 12   (D) 12 or more

16

Name _____ Date _____

Fill in the circle with the letter of the correct answer.

1. Which of these figures is a pyramid?

   (A)   (B)   (C)   (D)

2. Which of the following is *not* an odd number?

   (A) 5   (B) 19   (C) 17   (D) 4

3. Which of the shaded figures is *not* the base of the pyramid?

   (A)   (B)   (C)   (D)

For exercises 4–6, mark the letter of the group of words that means the same as the underlined words.

4. The truck weighed at least 2 tons.

   (A) 4,000 pounds or more   (C) 400 pounds or more
   (B) 4,000 pounds or less   (D) 400 pounds or less

5. After the party, there were over a dozen muffins left over.

   (A) fewer than 12   (C) about 13
   (B) more than 10   (D) 13 or more

6. The puppy weighed 1.5 pounds.

   (A) 15 pounds   (C) one and one-half pounds
   (B) one and one-fifth pound   (D) one and one-fifth pounds

122

Name _____ Date _____

For exercises 7–8, fill in the circle with the letter of the correct answer. Explain why you made your choice.

7. In these sentences, which number is an estimate?

   One dollar is worth the same as 5 dimes and 2 quarters.

   Lunch will cost about 3 dollars.

   (A) One _____
   (B) 5 _____
   (C) 2 _____
   (D) 3 _____

8. There are two seventh-grade classes. Each class has 28 students. Which picture best shows the math in the sentence?

   (A) _____

   (B) _____

For exercise 9, write your answer on the lines provided.

9. Melanie has 2 more bracelets than her sister Josie. Write a sentence using words, numerals, and symbols, that has the same meaning.

   _____

For exercise 10, draw a picture to show the math.

10. The carpet was 12 feet long and 10 feet wide.

Chapter 1 Test (Alternate Form)   **123**

For exercises 7–8, fill in the circle with the letter of the correct answer.
Explain why you made your choice. **Sample explanations are provided.**

7. In these sentences, which number is an estimate?
   One United States dollar has the same value as 10 dimes or 4 quarters.
   A United States dollar is worth about 0.6 of an English pound.

   (A) one   The word *about* tells me that 0.6 is an estimate.

   (B) 10   _____

   (C) 4   _____

   (D) 0.6   _____

8. There are four sixth-grade classes. Each class has 28 students.
   Which picture best shows the math in the sentence?

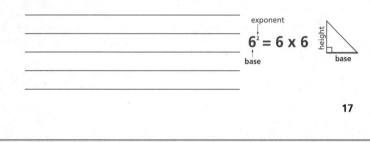

   I need 4 groups of 28, not 28

   placed into 4 equal groups.

   _____

   _____

For exercises 9–10, write your answer on the lines provided. **Sample answers are provided.**

9. Fran's score was 5 points less than Katy's score. Write a sentence
   using words, numerals, and symbols, that has the same meaning.

   Fran's score = Katy's score − 5

10. Explain, using words or pictures, at least two mathematical meanings
    of the word *base*.

    _____

    _____

    _____

    _____

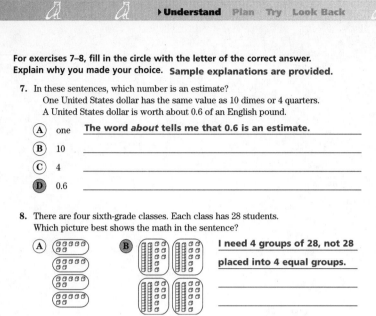

exponent

$6^2 = 6 \times 6$

base

height

base

17

Ideas for Struggling Learners

- Students can decode by writing a numeral whenever they come across a number written in words.

- Students can point to and read aloud passages that may be challenging.

- Students can use the margins to jot down important information.

- Students can work in pairs to take turns. One reads a question and the other paraphrases it. When they're sure they understand the questions, they can work independently to complete the test.

Answers for Alternate Form Test

1. B	**4.** A
2. D	**5.** D
3. C	**6.** C

7. D; Possible explanation: The word *about* tells me that 3 is an estimate.

8. B; Possible explanation: I need two groups of 28, not 28 placed in 2 equal groups.

9. Sample answer:
the number of bracelets Josie has + 2 = the number of bracelets Melanie has

10.

12 feet

10 feet

Chapter 2

An African Safari

Finding Exactly What You Need

An African Safari

Finding Exactly What You Need

On Safari with Family Safaris

See·······
· the migration of the wildebeest
· tree-climbing lions
· the world's largest living bird
· elephants, zebras, giraffes
· and much, much more!

© Great Source. Copying is prohibited.

18

Using Pages 18–19

Guiding the Reading

Have students read these two pages independently. Use the copymaster on page 117 of this book to help guide their reading.

Point out to students that, unlike most words, the word *wildebeest* is spelled the same when it is singular (one wildebeest) or plural (many wildebeest).

Connecting to the Theme

These are optional ideas for connecting to the theme of the African safari as you do this chapter.

• Divide your students into small groups. Have each group research and give a report on a different African animal.

• Have your students play one of the variations of the mancala game played in East Africa. See the website listed on page 19.

Bibliography

There are many books on each African animal. You and/or your students can easily find these books in the library. Here are a few to get you started.

Darling, Cathy. *Lions: A Carolrhoda Nature Watch Book*. Minneapolis, MN: Carolrhoda Books, Inc. 2000.

Arnold, Caroline. *Giraffe*. New York: William Morrow & Co., Inc., 1987.

Walker, Sally M. *Hippos*. Minneapolis, MN: Carolrhoda Books, Inc., 1998.

In this chapter, you will go on an African safari. As you travel, you'll be collecting all kinds of interesting information about Africa and its many animals. You'll also practice finding information that is shown in graphs, diagrams, and pictures. And, you'll learn how to find just the information you need in order to solve a math problem. This will help you with the first step of the four-step problem-solving method: **Understand**.

Safari means *journey* in Swahili, an African language. In English it has come to mean *a journey to view wildlife in Africa*. One Swahili word you hear often on a safari is *jambo*. Jambo means *hello* and total strangers will say it to you as you pass them.

▸ You will see many *kopjes* on the safari. Kopjes are rocky outcrops made up of very old granite. Predators like the cheetah use them as look-outs.

▴ Researchers usually name lion prides for the area where they live. For example, one pride is named Maasai Kopje because the pride lives around the Maasai Kopje. A researcher names a lion the first time he or she sees it. Its name is made up of the initials of the name of the pride and a letter or number for its unique identification. For example, the lion MKL was born in the Maasai Kopje pride and the letter L distinguishes it from other lions in that pride.

▸ It may surprise you that in some areas of Africa the lions climb trees.

19

Websites

Serengeti: The National Park's Official Site
http://www.serengeti.org/
   The official site of the Serengeti. You can even play a game that involves the sounds of animals in the Serengeti.

The Game of Bao, or Mancala in East Africa
http://www.driedger.ca/mankala/Man-2.html
   Information on variations of the Mancala game played in East Africa.

Sample Answers for Reading Guide

1. Africa
2. go on an African safari
3. Sample answers: the migration of the wildebeest, tree-climbing lions, the world's largest living bird, elephants, zebras, giraffes, cheetahs, kopjes
4. an African language
5. journey
6. hello
7. rocky outcrops made up of very old granite
8. A researcher names a lion the first time he or she sees it.
9. The lion was born in the Masai Kopje pride. L distinguishes it from the other lions in that pride.
10. yes
11. Understand

Chapter 2 Reading Guide for Pages 18-19

Name _____ Date _____

1. Which continent will you visit in this chapter? _____

2. What will you do while you are there?
   _____

3. Name three things you will see on the safari.
   _____
   _____
   _____

4. What is Swahili? _____

5. What is the meaning of the Swahili word *safari*? _____

6. What is the meaning of the Swahili word *jambo*? _____

7. What are *kopjes*?
   _____

8. When a lion pride is being studied, who gives each lion its name? When?

9. If a lion has been given the name MKL, what does that name mean?
   _____
   _____

10. Is it possible for a lion to climb a tree? _____

11. Which problem-solving step will you practice in Chapter 2? _____

117

Objectives

Identify the graph that shows the information you need.

Use graphs to find specific information.

Using Math at Hand

References to handbook items appear with the following exercises.

Exercises 1–7 Items 276–278 (Circle Graphs; Single-Line Graphs)

Exercise 3 Items 189–191 (Percent)

Exercise 4 Items 005–007 (Large Numbers)

Exercise 5 Item 008 (Comparing Whole Numbers)

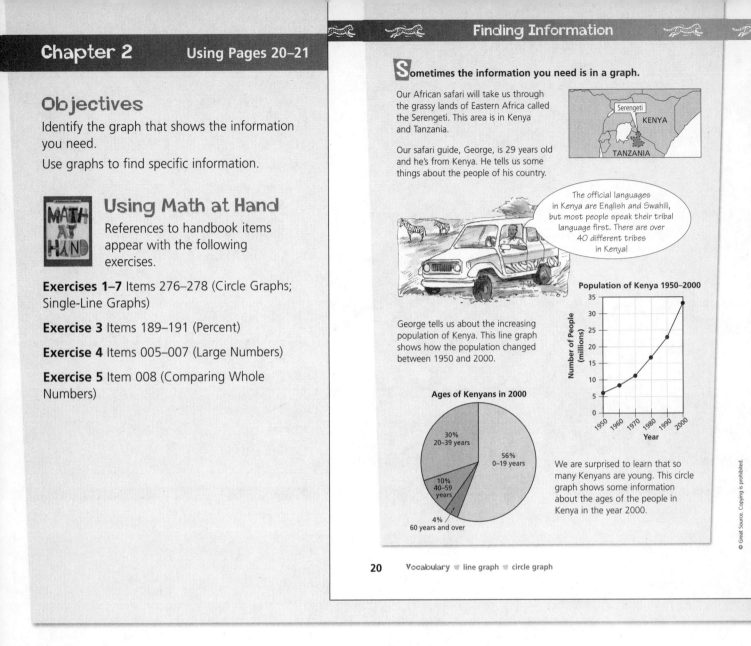

Sometimes the information you need is in a graph.

Our African safari will take us through the grassy lands of Eastern Africa called the Serengeti. This area is in Kenya and Tanzania.

Our safari guide, George, is 29 years old and he's from Kenya. He tells us some things about the people of his country.

The official languages in Kenya are English and Swahili, but most people speak their tribal language first. There are over 40 different tribes in Kenya!

George tells us about the increasing population of Kenya. This line graph shows how the population changed between 1950 and 2000.

Ages of Kenyans in 2000

30% 20–39 years
56% 0–19 years
10% 40–59 years
4% 60 years and over

Population of Kenya 1950–2000

We are surprised to learn that so many Kenyans are young. This circle graph shows some information about the ages of the people in Kenya in the year 2000.

20   Vocabulary ▼ line graph ▼ circle graph

Beginning the Lesson

Read the introduction yourself or ask a volunteer to read it aloud.

Use the following questions to check students' understanding of the introduction.

- *Who is the tour guide for the safari and how old is he?* (George; 29)
- *What information is shown in the line graph?* (The population of Kenya in the years from 1950 through 2000.)
- *Is the population increasing (getting larger) or decreasing (getting smaller)?* (increasing)
- *What information is given in the circle graph?* (It tells about the ages of the people of Kenya in the year 2000.)
- *What does it mean to be age 0?* (The person has not yet had his or her first birthday.)

Exercises: Getting Started

Have students work independently or in small groups on the exercises on page 21.

You may wish to work through exercise 1 with the whole class. *What was the population of Kenya in 1970?* (about 11 million) *If the population doubled, what would be the new population?* (about 22 million) *What was the population in 2000?* (about 33 million) *How does 22 million compare to 33 million?* (22 million < 33 million) *Which words should we put in the blank in exercise 1?* (more than) *Which graph gave you the information you needed to do this exercise?* (line graph) Check to be sure students have circled the correct answers.

Use the data from the graphs and circle the correct answer. ◂MAH 276–278

1. The population of Kenya _____ doubled between 1970 and 2000.

   a. The term in the blank should be (more than) less than

   b. To decide, I used the (line graph) circle graph

2. The population of Kenya in 1980 was _____ 15,000,000.

   a. The term in the blank should be (more than) less than

   b. To decide, I used the (line graph) circle graph

3. In 2000, _____ 50% of the people in Kenya were under 20 years old. ◂MAH 189–191

   a. The term in the blank should be (more than) less than

   b. To decide, I used the line graph (circle graph)

4. _____ thirty million people lived in Kenya in 2000. ◂MAH 005–007

   a. The term in the blank should be (more than) less than

   b. To decide, I used the (line graph) circle graph

5. Kenya is about the size of Texas. In 2000, the population of Texas was 20,852,000. This is _____ the population of Kenya in the same year. ◂MAH 008

   a. The term in the blank should be more than (less than)

   b. To decide, I used the (line graph) circle graph

6. In 2000, _____ a quarter of the people of Kenya were 40 or over.

   a. The term in the blank should be more than (less than)

   b. To decide, I used the line graph (circle graph)

7. In 2000, _____ half of the people in Kenya were younger than the safari guide. (**HINT:** You'll find the safari guide's age on page 20.)

   a. The term in the blank should be (more than) less than

   b. To decide, I used the line graph (circle graph)

more ▶

21

Vocabulary

circle graph   line graph

Direct students to the vocabulary words at the bottom of page 20. Have them find each word on the page and circle it. Then have them go to the Vocabulary section of the student book, starting on page 108. Ask them to write and/or illustrate a definition for each word.

Encourage students to use *Math at Hand*, a dictionary, or a math textbook to help them write their definitions.

If some students need help writing correct definitions, you may wish to share with them the sample definitions given in this teacher's guide starting on page 108.

Optional Follow Up

The circle graph on page 20 shows that more than $\frac{1}{2}$ of the population of Kenya is under 20 years old. Ask: *Do you think that more or less than $\frac{1}{2}$ of the population of the United States is under 20?* Have students find out by using an almanac or the U.S. Census Bureau website (www.census.gov).

Exercise 5 states that Kenya and Texas are about the same size. Have students look up the actual areas of Kenya and Texas.

Discussing the Exercises

When going over the exercises, allow time for class discussion.

1–7. *How did you decide whether to use the line graph or the circle graph?* (If the problem is about population figures, use the line graph. If the problem is about ages of people in Kenya in 2000, use the circle graph.)

3. *What fraction is equivalent to 50%?* ($\frac{1}{2}$)

5. Be sure students are able to correctly read the population of Texas. (twenty million, eight hundred fifty-two thousand)

6. *What percent is equivalent to* a quarter? (25%) Point out the relationship between per*cents* and *cents*.

7. *How did you decide on your answer?* (Some students may reason that 56% is more than 50%, or $\frac{1}{2}$. Others may just look at the graph and see that the section for 0–19 is more than $\frac{1}{2}$ of the circle. Encourage students to see both ways of getting the correct answer.

Objectives

Scan text for key words that might be clues to the answers to questions.

Use charts and graphs to find specific information.

Using Math at Hand

References to handbook items appear after the following exercises.

Exercises 15–17 Item 254 (Tallies)

Exercise 17 Item 262 (Mode)

Exercises 18–21 Item 282 (Line Plots)

Exercise 21 Item 258 (Outliers)

Sometimes, you need to read through paragraphs to find the information you need.

The ostrich holds several world records.

The ostrich is the world's largest living bird. But it does not fly. It is too big and too heavy. An adult ostrich is about 7 feet tall and weighs about 250 pounds.

An ostrich can run faster than any other 2-legged animal. It can accelerate to 40 miles per hour in less than 2 seconds. Ostriches do not tire easily and can keep up a pace of 30 miles per hour for 20 minutes or longer. When you watch ostriches run, they look like they are skimming across the surface of the ground.

The ostrich egg is white, slightly oval, and about 8 inches long. It is the biggest egg in the world. Each ostrich egg is equal in volume to about 2 dozen chicken eggs.

Refer to the paragraphs about ostriches to answer questions 8–14. Exercise 8 has a hint.

8. About how tall is the average adult ostrich? **7 feet**

9. For how long is an ostrich able to keep up a speed of 30 miles per hour?
   20 minutes or more

10. About how much does the average adult ostrich weigh? **250 lb**

11. Can an ostrich ever reach a speed of more than 30 miles per hour? **Yes**

12. How many chicken eggs are about the same volume as 1 ostrich egg? **24**

13. About how long is an ostrich egg? **8 in.**

14. What three world records are held by the ostrich?
    largest living bird, fastest-running 2-legged animal, largest egg

22   Vocabulary ▼ speed ▼ miles per hour (mph) ▼ volume

Exercises: Getting Started

Have students work independently or in small groups on the exercises on pages 22–23. Be sure students understand that they need to use the text at the top of the page to answer the questions on page 22.

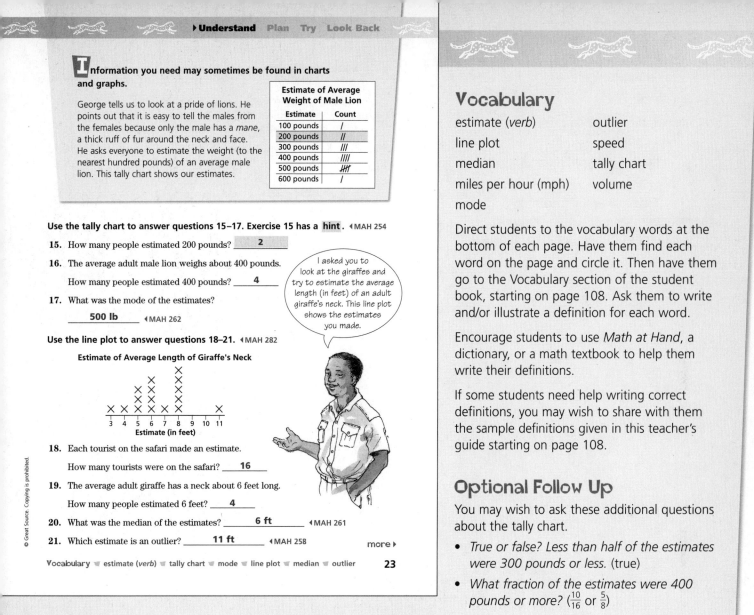

Information you need may sometimes be found in charts and graphs.

George tells us to look at a pride of lions. He points out that it is easy to tell the males from the females because only the male has a *mane*, a thick ruff of fur around the neck and face. He asks everyone to estimate the weight (to the nearest hundred pounds) of an average male lion. This tally chart shows our estimates.

Estimate of Average Weight of Male Lion	
Estimate	Count
100 pounds	/
200 pounds	//
300 pounds	///
400 pounds	////
500 pounds	/////
600 pounds	/

Use the tally chart to answer questions 15–17. Exercise 15 has a hint. ◀MAH 254

15. How many people estimated 200 pounds? __2__

16. The average adult male lion weighs about 400 pounds.

    How many people estimated 400 pounds? __4__

17. What was the mode of the estimates?

    __500 lb__ ◀MAH 262

I asked you to look at the giraffes and try to estimate the average length (in feet) of an adult giraffe's neck. This line plot shows the estimates you made.

Use the line plot to answer questions 18–21. ◀MAH 282

Estimate of Average Length of Giraffe's Neck

```
                    X
                    X
        X   X       X
        X   X   X   X
    X   X   X   X   X
X   X   X   X   X   X           X
3   4   5   6   7   8   9  10  11
        Estimate (in feet)
```

18. Each tourist on the safari made an estimate.

    How many tourists were on the safari? __16__

19. The average adult giraffe has a neck about 6 feet long.

    How many people estimated 6 feet? __4__

20. What was the median of the estimates? __6 ft__ ◀MAH 261

21. Which estimate is an outlier? __11 ft__ ◀MAH 258

more ▶

Vocabulary ▾ estimate (*verb*) ▾ tally chart ▾ mode ▾ line plot ▾ median ▾ outlier   **23**

© Great Source. Copying is prohibited.

Vocabulary

estimate (*verb*)	outlier
line plot	speed
median	tally chart
miles per hour (mph)	volume
mode	

Direct students to the vocabulary words at the bottom of each page. Have them find each word on the page and circle it. Then have them go to the Vocabulary section of the student book, starting on page 108. Ask them to write and/or illustrate a definition for each word.

Encourage students to use *Math at Hand*, a dictionary, or a math textbook to help them write their definitions.

If some students need help writing correct definitions, you may wish to share with them the sample definitions given in this teacher's guide starting on page 108.

Optional Follow Up

You may wish to ask these additional questions about the tally chart.

- *True or false? Less than half of the estimates were 300 pounds or less.* (true)

- *What fraction of the estimates were 400 pounds or more?* ($\frac{10}{16}$ or $\frac{5}{8}$)

Discussing the Exercises

When going over the exercises, allow time for class discussion.

8–14. When going over these exercises, you may wish to share some time-saving tips with students.

- When a question asks about height or length, scan the paragraphs for words like *inches, feet, yards,* and so on.

- When a question asks about time, scan the paragraphs for *minutes, hours, seconds.*

17. *What is the mode of a set of data?* (the piece of data that occurs most often)

18. *How do you determine the number of tourists?* (Count the Xs.)

20. *What is the median?* (the middle number or the average of the two middle numbers if there are an even number of pieces of data)

21. *What is an outlier?* (a piece of data that seems to float too far out at one end of the range)

© Great Source. Copying is prohibited.

Objective

Find information in a Venn diagram.

Using Math at Hand

References to handbook items appear with the following exercises.

Exercises 22–35 Item 283 (Venn Diagrams)

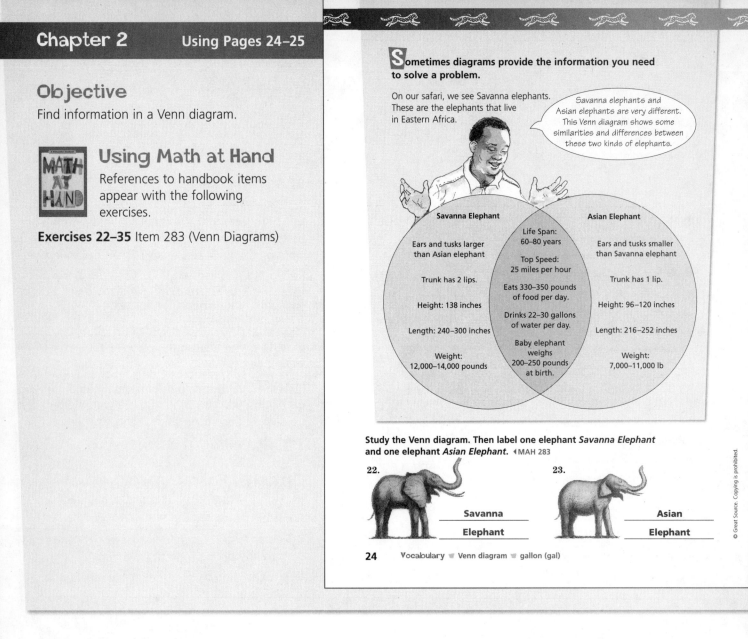

Sometimes diagrams provide the information you need to solve a problem.

On our safari, we see Savanna elephants. These are the elephants that live in Eastern Africa.

Savanna elephants and Asian elephants are very different. This Venn diagram shows some similarities and differences between these two kinds of elephants.

Savanna Elephant

Ears and tusks larger than Asian elephant

Trunk has 2 lips.

Height: 138 inches

Length: 240–300 inches

Weight: 12,000–14,000 pounds

Life Span: 60–80 years

Top Speed: 25 miles per hour

Eats 330–350 pounds of food per day.

Drinks 22–30 gallons of water per day.

Baby elephant weighs 200–250 pounds at birth.

Asian Elephant

Ears and tusks smaller than Savanna elephant

Trunk has 1 lip.

Height: 96–120 inches

Length: 216–252 inches

Weight: 7,000–11,000 lb

Study the Venn diagram. Then label one elephant *Savanna Elephant* **and one elephant** *Asian Elephant.* ◀MAH 283

22.

_____ Savanna

_____ Elephant

23.

_____ Asian

_____ Elephant

24   Vocabulary ▼ Venn diagram ▼ gallon (gal)

Beginning the Lesson

Read the introduction yourself or ask a volunteer to read it aloud.

Use the following questions to check students' understanding of the introduction.

- *Which adult elephant weighs more, the Savanna elephant or the Asian elephant?* (the Savanna elephant)

- *Which baby elephant weighs more?* (They weigh about the same.)

Exercises: Getting Started

Have students work independently or in small groups on the exercises on pages 24–25.

For exercises 24–31, use the Venn diagram from page 24. Write *true*, *false*, or *can't tell*.   ◀MAH 283

____true____ 24. Adult Savanna elephants weigh more than Asian elephants.

____false____ 25. Asian elephants weigh more than 300 pounds at birth.

____true____ 26. Asian elephants drink at least 22 gallons of water per day.

____true____ 27. It is possible for a Savanna elephant and an Asian elephant to be the same length.

__can't tell__ 28. An elephant could run 25 miles in one hour.

____false____ 29. All Asian elephants live longer than all Savanna elephants.

____false____ 30. Savanna elephants and Asian elephants have the same kind of trunks.

____false____ 31. All Asian elephant babies are smaller than all African elephant babies.

For exercises 32–35, use the Venn diagram. Pick from the box a word that makes the sentence true.

| less than |
| likely |
| unlikely |
| greater than |

32. Elephants usually travel at a speed that is ___less than___ 25 miles per hour.

33. The weight of most adult elephants is ___greater than___ 7000 pounds.

34. If you see an elephant that is 125 inches tall, it is ___likely___ to be a Savanna elephant.

35. An elephant that is 100 inches tall, 240 inches long, and weighs 10,000 pounds is ___unlikely___ to be a Savanna elephant.

Did you know?
For a long time, scientists believed that there was only one species of African elephants. They now know that there are at least two species— the Savanna elephant and the Forest elephant. When people talk about African elephants, however, they are usually talking about Savanna elephants. Most people have never seen a Forest elephant, which lives in west and central Africa. They are much smaller than Savanna elephants and have smaller, rounded ears and straighter trunks.

Did you know?
If you ever watch an old Tarzan movie, take a good look at the elephants. These movies show Tarzan in Africa riding Asian elephants!

© Great Source. Copying is prohibited.

25

Vocabulary

gallon (gal)

Venn diagram

Direct students to the vocabulary words at the bottom of page 24. Have them find each word on the page and circle it. Then have them go to the Vocabulary section of the student book, starting on page 108. Ask them to write and/or illustrate a definition for each word.

Encourage students to use *Math at Hand*, a dictionary, or a math textbook to help them write their definitions.

If some students need help writing correct definitions, you may wish to share with them the sample definitions given in this teacher's guide starting on page 108.

Optional Follow Up

Have students write additional true/false questions that can be answered using the Venn diagram.

Discussing the Exercises

When going over the exercises, allow time for class discussion.

22–23. *How did you decide which of the elephants was a Savanna Elephant?* (Possible answer: The Savanna elephant has larger ears.)

28. *Why can't you tell that an elephant could run 25 miles in one hour?* (25 miles per hour is the *rate* at which they can run, but we don't know how *long* they can sustain that speed.)

© Great Source. Copying is prohibited.

Objectives

Recognize needed information in context.

Use a table to find specific information.

Using Math at Hand

References to handbook items appear with the following exercises.

Exercises 1–7 Item 267 (Data in Tables)

Most tables, graphs, and books give you more information than you need.

One of the most incredible sights you see on the safari is the annual Serengeti migration. The information on this page tells you about this amazing event and gives you some facts about the animals that take part in it.

The Serengeti Migration

This migration occurs each year. About one and a half million antelope, called wildebeest; about 200,000 Burchell's zebras; and about 500,000 Thompson's gazelle start travelling to take advantage of different weather conditions. These grass-eating animals spend the wet season on the plains and the dry season in the woodlands. The animals' hoofbeats sound like thunder. The earth shakes. Nothing, even a river full of crocodiles, can hold them back. Lions, leopards, and cheetahs follow along, ready to pounce on stray animals. Wild dogs and hyenas join, and vultures fly overhead.

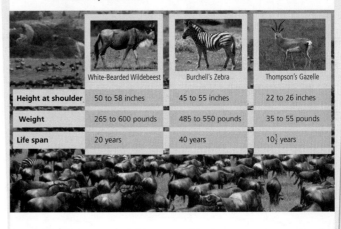

	White-Bearded Wildebeest	Burchell's Zebra	Thompson's Gazelle
Height at shoulder	50 to 58 inches	45 to 55 inches	22 to 26 inches
Weight	265 to 600 pounds	485 to 550 pounds	35 to 55 pounds
Life span	20 years	40 years	$10\frac{1}{2}$ years

26

Beginning the Lesson

Read the introduction yourself or ask a volunteer to read it aloud. Point out to students that wildebeest and gazelle are spelled the same whether singular (one wildebeest, one gazelle) or plural (many wildebeest, many gazelle).

Use the following question to check students' understanding of the introduction.

- *How often does the Serengeti migration occur?* (annually, that is, once a year)

- *Why does the migration occur?* (Grass-eating animals travel to the place where they can get food.)

Exercises: Getting Started

Have students work independently or in small groups on the exercises on page 27.

Before you can solve each problem, you need to find two or three pieces of data from page 26. Write the information you need. Exercise 1 has some hints. ◀ MAH 267

1. Do more zebras than gazelle take part in the Serengeti migration?

   about 200,000 zebras   about 500,000 gazelle

   _____   _____

2. Altogether about how many wildebeest, zebras, and gazelle take part in the migration?

   1.5 million wildebeest   **200,000 zebras**   **500,000 gazelle**

3. What is the difference between the maximum and minimum weights given for the wildebeest?

   600 lb   **265 lb**

   _____   _____

4. What is the range of heights given for the gazelle?

   22 in.   **26 in.**

   _____   _____

5. Which is greater, the maximum weight for the wildebeest or the maximum weight for the zebra?

   wildebeest: 600 lb   **zebra: 550 lb**

   _____   _____

6. Which of the 3 animals has the shortest minimum height?

   wildebeest: 50 in.   **zebra: 45 in.**   **gazelle: 22 in.**

   _____   _____   _____

7. Which of the 3 animals has the longest life span?

   wildebeest: 20 yr   **zebra: 40 yr**   **gazelle $10\frac{1}{2}$ yr**

   _____   _____   _____

Vocabulary ▼ maximum ▼ minimum ▼ range   **27**

Vocabulary

maximum

minimum

range

Direct students to the vocabulary words at the bottom of page 27. Have them find the words on the page and circle them. Then have them go to the Vocabulary section of the student book, starting on page 108. Ask them to write and/or illustrate a definition for each word.

Encourage students to use *Math at Hand*, a dictionary, or a math textbook to help them write their definition.

If some students need help writing the correct definition, you may wish to share with them the sample definition given in this teacher's guide starting on page 108.

Optional Follow Up

Have students make a bar graph showing the life spans of the three animals in the chart.

Discussing the Exercises

When going over the exercises, allow time for class discussion.

3. *What is the maximum?* (the greatest value) *the minimum?* (the least value)

Extending the Lesson: Solving the Problems

You may wish to have students use a separate piece of paper to solve the problems.

1. no
2. 2,200,000
3. 335 pounds
4. 4 inches
5. maximum weight for the wildebeest
6. gazelle
7. zebra

Objective

Decide when and where to look up needed information.

Using Math at Hand

References to handbook items appear with the following exercises.

Exercise 3 Item 486 (The Customary System of Measurement)

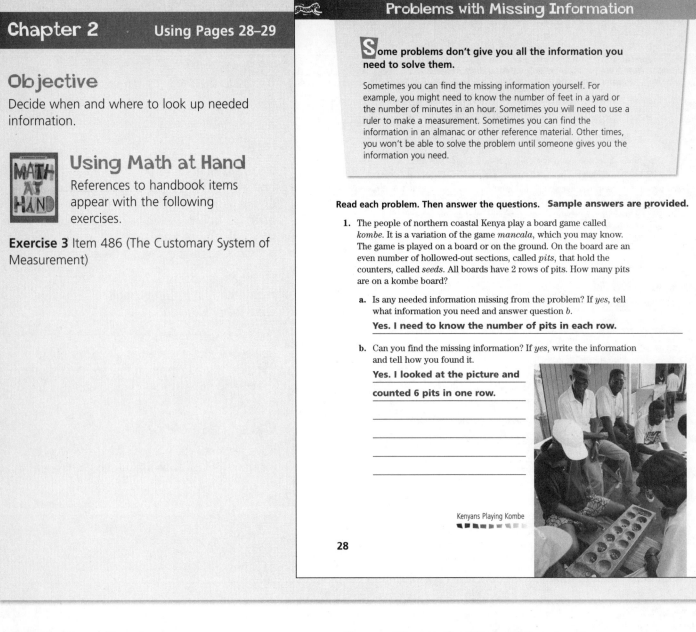

Some problems don't give you all the information you need to solve them.

Sometimes you can find the missing information yourself. For example, you might need to know the number of feet in a yard or the number of minutes in an hour. Sometimes you will need to use a ruler to make a measurement. Sometimes you can find the information in an almanac or other reference material. Other times, you won't be able to solve the problem until someone gives you the information you need.

Read each problem. Then answer the questions.   Sample answers are provided.

1. The people of northern coastal Kenya play a board game called *kombe*. It is a variation of the game *mancala*, which you may know. The game is played on a board or on the ground. On the board are an even number of hollowed-out sections, called *pits*, that hold the counters, called *seeds*. All boards have 2 rows of pits. How many pits are on a kombe board?

   a. Is any needed information missing from the problem? If *yes*, tell what information you need and answer question *b*.

   Yes. I need to know the number of pits in each row.

   b. Can you find the missing information? If *yes*, write the information and tell how you found it.

   Yes. I looked at the picture and

   counted 6 pits in one row.

   Kenyans Playing Kombe

28

Beginning the Lesson

Read the introduction yourself or ask a volunteer to read it aloud.

Exercises: Getting Started

Have students work independently or in small groups on the exercises on pages 28–29. Remind students that they may not be able to answer some questions in this section because they will not be able to find the needed information.

2. On a safari, trips to photograph game (*game runs*) are made twice a day, early in the morning and late in the afternoon. These are the times when the animals are active. How many game runs are made on our safari?

a. Is any needed information missing from the problem? If *yes*, tell what information you need and answer question *b*.

Yes. I need to know the number of days on safari.

b. Can you find the missing information? If *yes*, write the information and tell how you found it.

No.

3. At top speed, a cheetah can run about 70 miles per hour. But, that doesn't mean it can run 140 miles in two hours. A cheetah can keep up this top speed for only about 300 yards. Is 300 yards more or less than $\frac{1}{2}$ mile? ◂MAH 486

a. Is any needed information missing from the problem? If *yes*, tell what information you need and answer question *b*.

Yes. I need to know the number of yards in a half-mile.

b. Can you find the missing information? If *yes*, write the information and tell how you found it.

Yes. There are 1760 yards in a mile and 880 yards in a half-mile. I used the handbook.

Did you know?
The cheetah is built for speed! It has a long greyhound-like body with light bones. Its special claw pads and claws provide great traction. Large nostrils and lungs provide quick air intake. The shape of its eye gives the cheetah a wide-angle view of its surroundings.

more ▸

29

Optional Follow Up

Have each student choose a fact using a reference book or a website. Then have the student write a problem whose solution requires that fact, but does not include the fact. Have students exchange problems and try to find the necessary information needed to solve each other's problems.

Discussing the Exercises

When going over the exercises, allow time for class discussion.

Extending the Lesson: Solving the Problems

You may wish to have students use a separate piece of paper to solve the problems.

1. The board in the picture has 12 pits.

2. This problem cannot be solved. There is no way to find out the number of days for the safari.

3. 300 yards is less than $\frac{1}{2}$ mile.

Objective

Decide what information is needed and where to find it.

Materials

Rulers

Using Math at Hand

References to handbook items appear with the following exercises.

Exercise 4 Item 188 (Scale Drawing)

Exercise 5 Item 284 (Stem-and-Leaf Plots)

Exercise 7 Item 005 (Reading and Writing Large Numbers)

Sometimes you need to do something with the information you have and sometimes you need to look up missing information.

Read each problem. Then answer the questions. Sample answers are provided.

4. The hippo in the picture is actually 11 feet long. What is the ratio of the length of the picture to the actual length of the hippo? ◄MAH 188

Did you know?
Scientists used to think that hippos were related to pigs. New research suggests that they are actually more closely related to whales and dolphins.

a. Is any needed information missing from the problem? If *yes*, tell what information you need and answer question *b*.

Yes. I need the length of the picture and the number of inches in a foot.

b. Can you find the missing information? If *yes*, write it and tell how you found it.

Yes. I measured and the picture is $3\frac{1}{2}$ inches long.

I know that 1 ft = 12 in.

5. The stem-and-leaf plot shows the ages of all the tourists on the safari with George. How many of the tourists are older than George? ◄MAH 284

Ages of Tourists on Safari

0	9
1	0 1 1 3 4
2	9
3	5 6 8
4	3 5 8
5	1 2
6	5

Key: 6|5 = 65 years old

a. Is any needed information missing from the problem? If *yes*, tell what you need and answer question *b*.

Yes. I need George's age.

b. Can you find the missing information? If *yes*, write the information and tell how you found it.

Yes. George is 20 years old. I found George's age on page 20.

30 Vocabulary ⫶ ratio ⫶ stem-and-leaf plot

© Great Source. Copying is prohibited.

Exercises: Getting Started

Have students work independently or in small groups on the exercises on pages 30–31.

© Great Source. Copying is prohibited.

6. Near the end of the trip, George takes the group to Olduvai Gorge. Olduvai Gorge is called the *Crater of Mankind* because many archaeological discoveries were made there. In 1911, a German professor was looking for butterflies and found fossil bones. How many years ago was that?

   a. Is any needed information missing from the problem? If *yes*, tell what information you need and answer question *b*.

      Yes. What year is it now?

   b. Can you find the missing information? If *yes*, write the information and tell how you found it.

      Yes. I know that this is (current year).

   _____

7. Olduvai Gorge is most famous for a 1959 discovery. Fossil fragments of a skull were found. Scientists say that it is the skull of a prehistoric man from about 1,800,000 years ago. Do scientists think the skull is more than 2 million years old? ◀ MAH 005

   a. Is any needed information missing from the problem? If *yes*, tell what information you need and answer question *b*.

      No.

   b. Can you find the missing information? If *yes*, write the information and tell how you found it.

   _____

   _____

8. In 1974, some tooth fossils were found. Scientists believe the fossils are about 2,400,000 years old. How many centuries old do scientists think the fossils are?

   a. Is any needed information missing from the problem? If *yes*, tell what information you need and answer question *b*.

      Yes. How many years are in a century?

   b. Can you find the missing information? If *yes*, write the information and tell how you found it.

      Yes. The handbook says that there are 100 years in a century.

   _____

more ▶

31

Vocabulary

ratio

stem-and-leaf plot

Direct students to the vocabulary words at the bottom of page 30. Have them find the words on the page and circle them. Then have them go to the Vocabulary section of the student book, starting on page 108. Ask them to write and/or illustrate a definition for each word.

Encourage students to use *Math at Hand*, a dictionary, or a math textbook to help them write their definition.

If some students need help writing correct definitions, you may wish to share with them the sample definitions given in this teacher's guide starting on page 108.

Discussing the Exercises

When going over the exercises, allow time for class discussion.

5. If students are not sure how to find George's age, tell them to look back at page 20.

7. Answers may vary, since some students may consider the missing information to be the way to write 2 million as a numeral. (2,000,000)

Extending the Lesson: Solving the Problems

You may wish to have students use a separate piece of paper to solve the problems.

4. $3\frac{1}{2}$ to 132

5. 9 tourists

6. Answer will depend on the current year.

7. no

8. 24,000 centuries

Objectives

Read a circle graph and a bar graph.

Decide what information is needed and where to find it.

Using Math at Hand

References to handbook items appear with the following exercises.

Exercise 9 Item 276 (Circle Graphs)

Exercise 10 Item 168 (Multiplying a Whole Number by a Fraction)

Exercise 12 Items 272 and 274 (Bar Graphs)

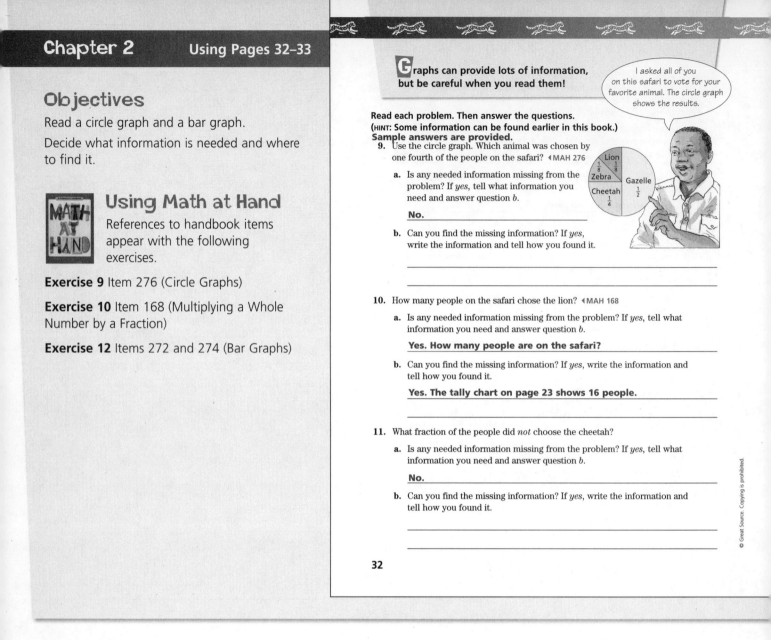

Graphs can provide lots of information, but be careful when you read them!

I asked all of you on this safari to vote for your favorite animal. The circle graph shows the results.

Read each problem. Then answer the questions.
(HINT: Some information can be found earlier in this book.)
Sample answers are provided.

9. Use the circle graph. Which animal was chosen by one fourth of the people on the safari? ◄MAH 276

  a. Is any needed information missing from the problem? If *yes*, tell what information you need and answer question *b*.

  No.

  b. Can you find the missing information? If *yes*, write the information and tell how you found it.

  _____

  _____

10. How many people on the safari chose the lion? ◄MAH 168

  a. Is any needed information missing from the problem? If *yes*, tell what information you need and answer question *b*.

  Yes. How many people are on the safari?

  b. Can you find the missing information? If *yes*, write the information and tell how you found it.

  Yes. The tally chart on page 23 shows 16 people.

  _____

11. What fraction of the people did *not* choose the cheetah?

  a. Is any needed information missing from the problem? If *yes*, tell what information you need and answer question *b*.

  No.

  b. Can you find the missing information? If *yes*, write the information and tell how you found it.

  _____

  _____

32

Exercises: Getting Started

Have students work independently or in small groups on the exercises on pages 32–33.

George works for a company called Family Safaris. This company advertises safaris to people all over North America. This bar graph shows the number of children and adults from the United States, Canada, and Mexico who have taken a safari with George this year.

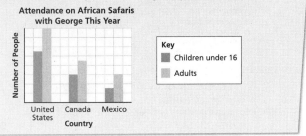

Attendance on African Safaris with George This Year

Key
- Children under 16
- Adults

Use this graph for exercises 12–13.

12. Did more adults than children from the United States go on a safari with George this year? ◀MAH 272, 274

  a. Is any needed information missing from the problem? If *yes*, tell what information you need and answer question *b*.

    No. _____

  b. Can you find the missing information? If *yes*, write the information and tell how you found it.

    _____

    _____

13. How many more people from the United States than from Canada went on a safari with George?

  a. Is any needed information missing from the problem? If *yes*, tell what information you need and answer question *b*.

    Yes. What numbers should label the vertical axis?

  b. Can you find the missing information? If *yes*, write the information and tell how you found it.

    No. _____

    _____

Vocabulary ▾ double-bar graph

33

Vocabulary
double-bar graph

Direct students to the vocabulary term at the bottom of page 33. Have them find the term on the page and circle it. Then have them go to the Vocabulary section of the student book, starting on page 108. Ask them to write and/or illustrate a definition for the term.

Encourage students to use *Math at Hand*, a dictionary, or a math textbook to help them write their definition.

If some students need help writing the correct definition, you may wish to share with them the sample definition given in the Vocabulary section of this teacher's guide starting on page 108.

Discussing the Exercises

When going over the exercises, allow time for class discussion.

9–11. Help students to understand that circle graphs do not usually provide answers to questions beginning with *How many* ... These kinds of questions require knowing how many people (or items) make up the entire group.

10–11. If students are not sure how to find out the number of people on the safari, tell them to look at the line plot on page 23 or the stem-and-leaf plot on page 30.

13. Students may want to assume that each square on the graph represents 1 person. Point out that you cannot assume this and that labels are necessary. *Why would it not make sense that each square stands for 1 person?* (The bar for children from the United States would show $5\frac{1}{2}$ children, which does not make sense.)

Extending the Lesson: Solving the Problems

You may wish to have students use a separate piece of paper to solve the problems.

  9. cheetah

10. 2 people

11. $\frac{3}{4}$

12. yes

13. This question cannot be answered without knowing the numbers that belong on the vertical axis.

Assessment

Two forms of the chapter test are available: the test on these two student pages and the test provided on the copymasters on pages 124–125 of this teacher's guide.

You can use these two forms of the test in the way that works best for you.

- Use one test as a pretest and the other as a posttest.
- Use one test as a practice test and one for assessment.
- Use one test as assessment and the other for a make-up test for students who were absent or who did poorly and need a chance to try again.

Fill in the circle with the letter of the correct answer.

1. According to the circle graph, which of these statements is *not* true?

   (A) Less than half of the chorus members are in grade 7.

   (B) More than half of the chorus members are in grade 8.

   (C) Less than a quarter of the chorus members are in grade 6.

   (D) More of the chorus members are in grade 8 than in any other grade.

Chorus Members

Grade 7 $\frac{3}{8}$ Grade 8 $\frac{1}{2}$ Grade 6 $\frac{1}{8}$

2. On which days were more than 25 students present in Room 204?

   (A) Monday, Wednesday, and Thursday

   (B) Tuesday, Wednesday, and Friday

   (C) Monday and Thursday

   (D) Tuesday and Friday

This Week's Attendance Room 204

Number of Students — Day (M T W Th F)

3. How many people were at the family reunion?

   (A) 27

   (B) 15

   (C) 36

   (D) 8

Ages of People at Family Reunion

0	2 3
1	5 6 8 9 9
2	0 1 1 4
3	1 1 2
4	0 1 4
5	2 7
6	1 4 5
7	2 3
8	5 6 9

Key: 1|5 = 15 years old

34

© Great Source. Copying is prohibited.

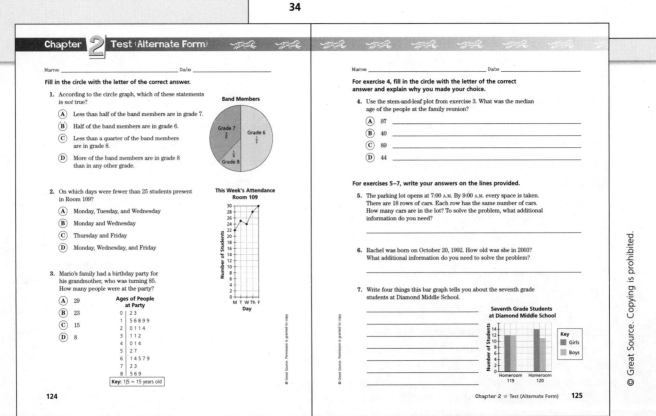

Chapter 2 Test (Alternate Form)

Name _____ Date _____

Fill in the circle with the letter of the correct answer.

1. According to the circle graph, which of these statements is *not* true?

   (A) Less than half of the band members are in grade 7.

   (B) Half of the band members are in grade 6.

   (C) Less than a quarter of the band members are in grade 8.

   (D) More of the band members are in grade 8 than in any other grade.

Band Members

Grade 7   Grade 6 $\frac{1}{2}$ Grade 8

2. On which days were fewer than 25 students present in Room 109?

   (A) Monday, Tuesday, and Wednesday

   (B) Monday and Wednesday

   (C) Thursday and Friday

   (D) Monday, Wednesday, and Friday

This Week's Attendance Room 109

Number of Students — Day (M T W Th F)

3. Mario's family had a birthday party for his grandmother, who was turning 85. How many people were at the party?

   (A) 29

   (B) 23

   (C) 15

   (D) 8

Ages of People at Party

0	2 3
1	5 6 8 9 9
2	0 1 1 4
3	1 1 2
4	0 1 4
5	2 7
6	1 4 5 7 9
7	2 3
8	5 6 9

Key: 1|5 = 15 years old

124

© Great Source. Permission is granted to copy.

Name _____ Date _____

For exercise 4, fill in the circle with the letter of the correct answer and explain why you made your choice.

4. Use the stem-and-leaf plot from exercise 3. What was the median age of the people at the family reunion?

   (A) 87 _____

   (B) 40 _____

   (C) 89 _____

   (D) 44 _____

For exercises 5–7, write your answers on the lines provided.

5. The parking lot opens at 7:00 A.M. By 9:00 A.M. every space is taken. There are 18 rows of cars. Each row has the same number of cars. How many cars are in the lot? To solve the problem, what additional information do you need?

6. Rachel was born on October 20, 1992. How old was she in 2003? What additional information do you need to solve the problem?

7. Write four things this bar graph tells you about the seventh grade students at Diamond Middle School.

Seventh Grade Students at Diamond Middle School

Number of Students — Homeroom 119, Homeroom 120

Key: Girls, Boys

Chapter 2 ✓ Test (Alternate Form)   125

© Great Source. Copying is prohibited.

For exercise 4, fill in the circle with the letter of the correct answer and explain why you made your choice.

4. Use the stem-and-leaf plot from exercise 3. What was the median age of the people at the family reunion?

   Ⓐ　32　**Sample explanation: There are 27 people, so the**

   Ⓑ　2　**14th person has the median age. I counted up from**

   Ⓒ　89　**the least number to the 14th number.**

   Ⓓ　27

For exercises 5–7, write your answer on the lines provided. **Sample answers are provided.**

5. Melissa returns 6 books that are overdue to the library. The fine is 5 cents per day for each book. To find the total fine that Melissa owes, what additional information do you need?

How many days overdue are the books?

6. Randy's bedroom is 10 feet long and 4 yards wide. To find out whether Randy's bedroom is more than 10 feet wide, what additional information do you need?

How many feet are in 1 yard?

7. Write 4 things this bar graph tells you about the eighth grade students at Vinebrook Middle School.

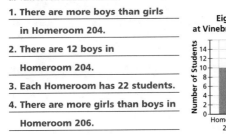

1. There are more boys than girls in Homeroom 204.

2. There are 12 boys in Homeroom 204.

3. Each Homeroom has 22 students.

4. There are more girls than boys in Homeroom 206.

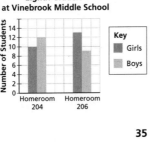

Eighth Graders at Vinebrook Middle School

Key
■ Girls
■ Boys

© Great Source. Copying is prohibited.

35

Answers for Alternate Form Test

1. D

2. B

3. A

4. B; Sample explanation: There are 29 people, so the 15th person has the median age. I counted up from the least number to the 15th number.

5. How many cars are in each row?

6. What month and day in 2003 are you talking about?

7. Sample answers:
   - Each homeroom has at least 24 students.
   - There are 12 boys in Homeroom 119.
   - There are more girls than boys in Homeroom 120.
   - There are more girls than boys in seventh grade.

© Great Source. Copying is prohibited.

Chapter **3**

The Red Lantern Musher
Making a Plan

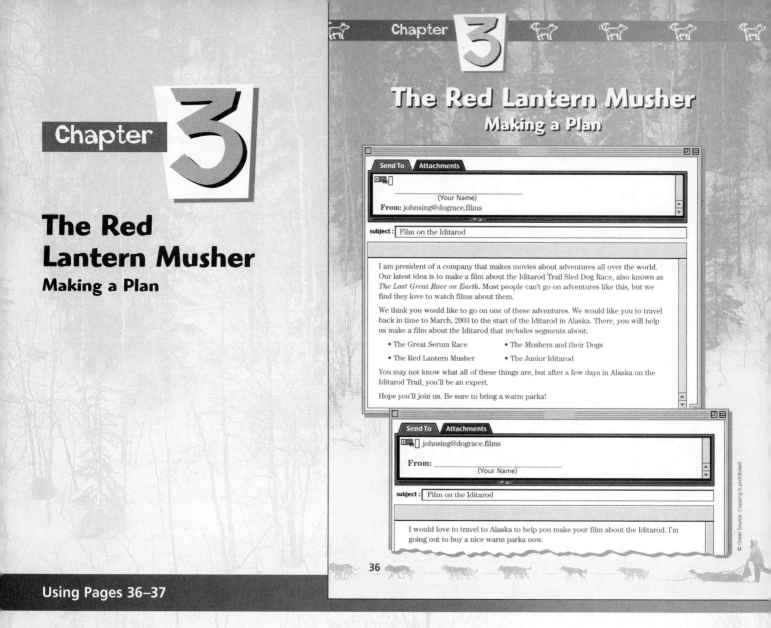

The Red Lantern Musher
Making a Plan

Send To | **Attachments**

_____
(Your Name)
From: johnsing@dograce.films

subject : Film on the Iditarod

I am president of a company that makes movies about adventures all over the world. Our latest idea is to make a film about the Iditarod Trail Sled Dog Race, also known as *The Last Great Race on Earth*. Most people can't go on adventures like this, but we find they love to watch films about them.

We think you would like to go on one of these adventures. We would like you to travel back in time to March, 2003 to the start of the Iditarod in Alaska. There, you will help us make a film about the Iditarod that includes segments about:

- The Great Serum Race
- The Mushers and their Dogs
- The Red Lantern Musher
- The Junior Iditarod

You may not know what all of these things are, but after a few days in Alaska on the Iditarod Trail, you'll be an expert.

Hope you'll join us. Be sure to bring a warm parka!

Send To | **Attachments**

johnsing@dograce.films

From: _____
(Your Name)

subject : Film on the Iditarod

I would love to travel to Alaska to help you make your film about the Iditarod. I'm going out to buy a nice warm parka now.

36

Using Pages 36–37

Guiding the Reading

Have students write their own names in the spaces provided in the e-mails. Then, ask students to try to read these two pages independently. Use the copymaster on page 118 of this book to help guide their reading.

Connecting to the Theme

These are optional ideas for connecting to the theme of the Iditarod as you use this chapter.

- The Iditarod starts in March. If you are lucky enough to be using this chapter at that time you can track the Iditarod daily on the Internet.

- On the Internet find the information about all the mushers for the most recent year. Have the students collect information about the mushers and organize it. For example, they might do a graph showing the ages of all the mushers.

- Create a play with your students about the Iditarod or The Great Serum Race.

Bibliography

Crisman, Ruth. *Racing the Iditarod Trail*. New York: Macmillan Publishing Company, 1993.
    A book about the Iditarod race.

Miller, Debbie S. *The Great Serum Race: Blazing the Iditarod Trail*. New York: Walker & Company, 2002.
    A book about the dog team relay to deliver serum to those with diphtheria in Nome, Alaska, in 1925. The Iditarod Race was started to remember this historic event that saved many lives.

Shahan, Sherry. *Racing Through the Snow: The Story of the Junior Iditarod*. Brookfield, Connecticut: The Millbrook Press, 1997.
    A book about the Junior Iditarod for kids who are under the age of 18.

A s you read about the Iditarod in this chapter, you will get an idea of all the work that goes on before the race. You'll see how making mental pictures and writing plans help people make the Iditarod such a great race. You'll also see how mental pictures can help you plan to solve math problems. You will get lots of practice using the first and second steps in the four-step problem-solving method: **Understand** and **Plan**.

Dog Team with Musher (driver) on Iditarod Trail

▲ The Athabascan Indians called their island hunting ground *Haiditarod*, which means *distant place*. Later, miners founded a town there and called it Iditarod. The original race trail goes through Iditarod and so the race came to be known as the Iditarod.

▲ While the exact route of the Iditarod is not always the same, it always begins in Anchorage and ends in Nome. It is said that the race is 1,049 miles long. The number 1,049 is symbolic. The race is always over 1,000 miles. The 49 stands for Alaska being the 49th state admitted to the United States.

▼ The Halfway Point Award is given to the leading musher at the halfway point. In 2003, Robert Sorlie won this award. His prize was 3,000 dollars worth of gold nuggets that are symbolic of the Iditarod Mining District.

▼ There are about 35 volunteer veterinarians who check the dogs during the Iditarod. At least three veterinarians are at each checkpoint to check the dogs. Each driver must also keep a dog-care diary, which the veterinarians read.

37

Sample Answers for Reading Guide

1. John Sing
2. the Iditarod Trail Sled Dog Race
3. March, 2003
4. distant place
5. The original race trail went through Iditarod.
6. the Halfway Point Award
7. 3,000 dollars worth of gold nuggets
8. It begins in Anchorage and ends in Nome.
9. 1,000
10. 3
11. Understand and Plan

Chapter 3 | **Reading Guide for Pages 36-37**

Name _____ Date _____

1. Who is inviting you to travel to Alaska? _____

2. In Alaska, you will be helping to make a film. What will be the film's topic?
_____

3. You will travel back in time. To what month and year will you go back?
_____

4. The Athabascan Indians called their island hunting ground *Haiditarod*. What does that word mean?
_____

5. Why is this famous race called the *Iditarod*?
_____

6. What award did Robert Sorlie win in 2003? _____

7. What was Robert Sorlie's prize in 2003?
_____

8. Where does the race begin and end?
_____

9. The race is always more than x miles long. What is the value of x?
_____

10. What is the minimum number of veterinarians at each checkpoint?
_____

11. Which problem-solving steps will you practice in Chapter 3?
_____

118

Websites

Iditarod
http://www.iditarod.com/
The official site of the Iditarod.

Dogsled.com–All the Adventure, None of the Frostbite
http://www.dogsled.com/
A wonderful site with lots of information about the Iditarod.

Objectives

Visualize the action in text.

Visualize the mathematical relationships in problems.

Using Math at Hand

References to handbook items appear with the following exercises.

Exercise 1 Item 136 (Multiplication)

Exercise 2 Item 144 (Division)

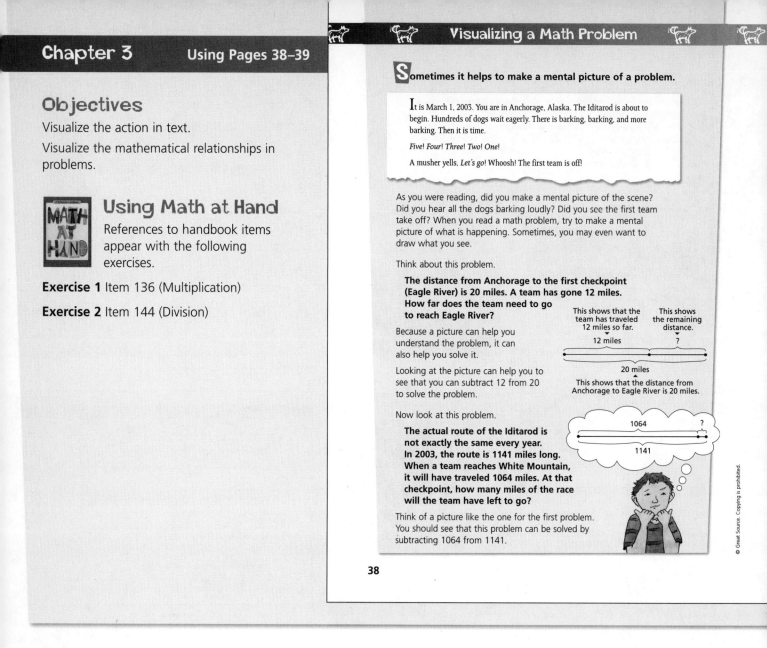

Sometimes it helps to make a mental picture of a problem.

It is March 1, 2003. You are in Anchorage, Alaska. The Iditarod is about to begin. Hundreds of dogs wait eagerly. There is barking, barking, and more barking. Then it is time.

Five! Four! Three! Two! One!

A musher yells, *Let's go!* Whoosh! The first team is off!

As you were reading, did you make a mental picture of the scene? Did you hear all the dogs barking loudly? Did you see the first team take off? When you read a math problem, try to make a mental picture of what is happening. Sometimes, you may even want to draw what you see.

Think about this problem.

The distance from Anchorage to the first checkpoint (Eagle River) is 20 miles. A team has gone 12 miles. How far does the team need to go to reach Eagle River?

Because a picture can help you understand the problem, it can also help you solve it.

Looking at the picture can help you to see that you can subtract 12 from 20 to solve the problem.

This shows that the team has traveled 12 miles so far.
12 miles

This shows the remaining distance.
?

20 miles
This shows that the distance from Anchorage to Eagle River is 20 miles.

Now look at this problem.

The actual route of the Iditarod is not exactly the same every year. In 2003, the route is 1141 miles long. When a team reaches White Mountain, it will have traveled 1064 miles. At that checkpoint, how many miles of the race will the team have left to go?

1064   ?
1141

Think of a picture like the one for the first problem. You should see that this problem can be solved by subtracting 1064 from 1141.

38

Beginning the Lesson

Read the introduction yourself or ask a volunteer to read it aloud.

Use the following questions to check students' understanding of the introduction.

- *Look at the picture for the first problem. How could you actually use that picture to solve the problem?* (Possible answer: Think: 12 + ? = 20, so ? must represent 8 miles.)

- If you plan to have students solve the problems on these pages, say, *Look at the picture for the second problem and use it to solve the problem.* (The picture shows the total distance, 1141 miles, and the distance traveled so far, 1064 miles. You can find *?* by subtracting 1064 from 1141 to get 77. There are 77 miles left to go.)

- *When you draw pictures like the ones on page 38, do you think you need to measure the segments in your drawing?* (No. The pictures, not the actual lengths, show the relationships.)

Exercises: Getting Started

Have students work independently or in small groups on the exercises on page 39.

Read the problem. Then follow the directions.

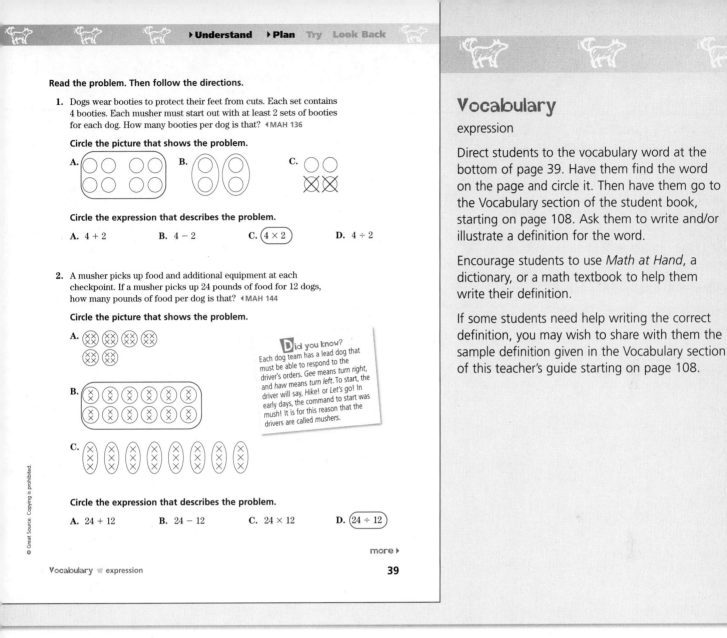

1. Dogs wear booties to protect their feet from cuts. Each set contains 4 booties. Each musher must start out with at least 2 sets of booties for each dog. How many booties per dog is that? ◂MAH 136

Circle the picture that shows the problem.

A. B. C.

Circle the expression that describes the problem.

A. 4 + 2   B. 4 − 2   C. (4 × 2)   D. 4 ÷ 2

2. A musher picks up food and additional equipment at each checkpoint. If a musher picks up 24 pounds of food for 12 dogs, how many pounds of food per dog is that? ◂MAH 144

Circle the picture that shows the problem.

A.

B.

C.

> **Did you know?**
> Each dog team has a lead dog that must be able to respond to the driver's orders. *Gee* means *turn right*, and *haw* means *turn left*. To start, the driver will say, *Hike!* or *Let's go!* In early days, the command to start was *mush!* It is for this reason that the drivers are called *mushers*.

Circle the expression that describes the problem.

A. 24 + 12   B. 24 − 12   C. 24 × 12   D. (24 ÷ 12)

more ▸

Vocabulary ▾ expression

Vocabulary

expression

Direct students to the vocabulary word at the bottom of page 39. Have them find the word on the page and circle it. Then have them go to the Vocabulary section of the student book, starting on page 108. Ask them to write and/or illustrate a definition for the word.

Encourage students to use *Math at Hand*, a dictionary, or a math textbook to help them write their definition.

If some students need help writing the correct definition, you may wish to share with them the sample definition given in the Vocabulary section of this teacher's guide starting on page 108.

Discussing the Exercises

When going over the exercises, allow time for class discussion.

1. *Using the numbers 2 and 4, what expression do you think matches picture B?* (4 ÷ 2) *Using the numbers 2 and 4, what expression do you think matches choice C?* (4 − 2) This exercise is a good example of why using key words without thinking isn't a useful strategy for solving a problem. Students who choose 4 ÷ 2 because *per* means division will get the wrong answer.

2. *Look at picture B (the correct picture). What does each X represent?* (one pound of food) *What does each circle represent?* (one dog)

Extending the Lesson: Solving the Problems

You may wish to have students solve the problems.

1. 8 booties per dog
2. 2 pounds of food per dog

Objectives

Read critically to match diagrams to text.

Understand the mathematical relationships in problems.

Using Math at Hand

References to handbook items appear with the following exercises.

Exercise 3 Item 260 (Mean)

Exercise 4 Items 131–132 (Subtracting with Regrouping)

Exercises 5–7 Item 168 (Multiplying a Whole Number by a Fraction)

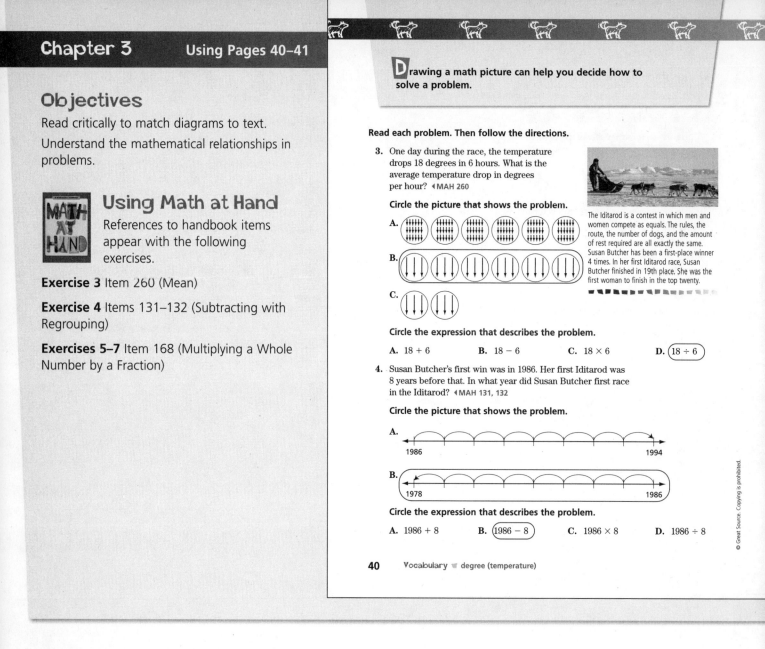

Drawing a math picture can help you decide how to solve a problem.

Read each problem. Then follow the directions.

3. One day during the race, the temperature drops 18 degrees in 6 hours. What is the average temperature drop in degrees per hour? ◀MAH 260

Circle the picture that shows the problem.

A.
B.
C.

Circle the expression that describes the problem.

A. 18 + 6   B. 18 − 6   C. 18 × 6   D. (18 ÷ 6)

4. Susan Butcher's first win was in 1986. Her first Iditarod was 8 years before that. In what year did Susan Butcher first race in the Iditarod? ◀MAH 131, 132

Circle the picture that shows the problem.

A.
   1986   1994

B.
   1978   1986

Circle the expression that describes the problem.

A. 1986 + 8   B. (1986 − 8)   C. 1986 × 8   D. 1986 ÷ 8

The Iditarod is a contest in which men and women compete as equals. The rules, the route, the number of dogs, and the amount of rest required are all exactly the same. Susan Butcher has been a first-place winner 4 times. In her first Iditarod race, Susan Butcher finished in 19th place. She was the first woman to finish in the top twenty.

40   Vocabulary ▾ degree (temperature)

Exercises: Getting Started

Have students work independently or in small groups on the exercises on pages 40–41. Remind them that the pictures they draw on page 41 should be simple. The important point is that they show the math.

5. The Iditarod rules state that each musher must carry an ax with a handle at least 22 inches long. One musher's ax handle was $1\frac{1}{2}$ times that long. How long was the handle? ◂MAH 168

Draw a picture that shows the problem.

Sample:

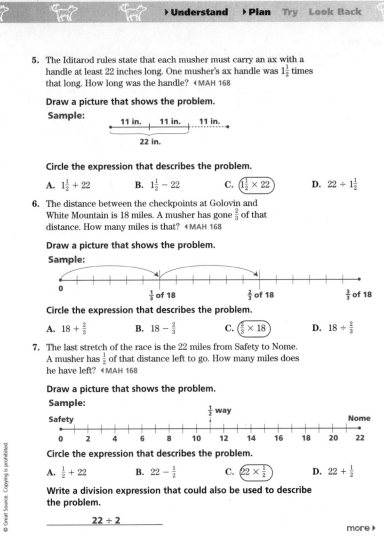

Circle the expression that describes the problem.

A. $1\frac{1}{2} + 22$ B. $1\frac{1}{2} - 22$ C. $\boxed{1\frac{1}{2} \times 22}$ D. $22 \div 1\frac{1}{2}$

6. The distance between the checkpoints at Golovin and White Mountain is 18 miles. A musher has gone $\frac{2}{3}$ of that distance. How many miles is that? ◂MAH 168

Draw a picture that shows the problem.

Sample:

0        $\frac{1}{3}$ of 18 $\frac{2}{3}$ of 18 $\frac{3}{3}$ of 18

Circle the expression that describes the problem.

A. $18 + \frac{2}{3}$ B. $18 - \frac{2}{3}$ C. $\boxed{\frac{2}{3} \times 18}$ D. $18 \div \frac{2}{3}$

7. The last stretch of the race is the 22 miles from Safety to Nome. A musher has $\frac{1}{2}$ of that distance left to go. How many miles does he have left? ◂MAH 168

Draw a picture that shows the problem.

Sample:

Safety $\frac{1}{2}$ way   Nome
0 2 4 6 8 10 12 14 16 18 20 22

Circle the expression that describes the problem.

A. $\frac{1}{2} + 22$ B. $22 - \frac{1}{2}$ C. $\boxed{22 \times \frac{1}{2}}$ D. $22 + \frac{1}{2}$

Write a division expression that could also be used to describe the problem.

$\underline{\hspace{2cm} 22 \div 2 \hspace{2cm}}$

more ▸

41

Vocabulary

degree (temperature)

Direct students to the vocabulary word at the bottom of page 40. Have them find the word on the page and circle it. Then have them go to the Vocabulary section of the student book, starting on page 108. Ask them to write and/or illustrate a definition for the word.

Encourage students to use *Math at Hand*, a dictionary, or a math textbook to help them write their definition.

If some students need help writing the correct definition, you may wish to share with them the sample definition given in the Vocabulary section of this teacher's guide starting on page 108.

Discussing the Exercises

When going over the exercises, allow time for class discussion.

4. *What expression do you think might be represented by picture A?* (1986 + 8)

5–7. Ask volunteers to show their drawings on the board. Discuss the fact that drawings do not need to look alike but should correctly show the math.

Extending the Lesson: Solving the Problems

You may wish to have students use a separate piece of paper to solve the problems.

3. 3 degrees

4. 1978

5. 33 inches

6. 12 miles

7. 11 miles

Objectives

Visualize the action in text.

Use a simpler problem to solve a more complex problem.

Using Math at Hand

References to handbook items appear with the following exercises.

Introduction Items 130 and 404 (Subtracting without Regrouping; Use Simpler Numbers)

Exercise 8 Item 151 (Another Way to Divide)

Exercise 9 Item 135 (Subtracting with Decimals)

Exercise 10 Item 139 (Two Ways to Multiply Whole Numbers)

You can use a simpler problem to help visualize a math problem.

Sometimes you can simplify the numbers in a problem to make it easier to plan a solution and check that it works. Then, you can go back and follow the same plan using the original numbers. ◄MAH 404

Example

Original problem First prize for the Iditarod in 2003 was $68,571. This was $56,571 more than for the 1973 Iditarod. What was the amount of the prize in 1973? ◄MAH 130

Think!

Simpler problem First prize in 2003 was $6. This was $5 more than in 1973. What was the amount of the prize in 1973?

Diagram of simpler problem

How to solve simpler problem

$5 more than 1973

$$\boxed{\$}\boxed{\$}\boxed{\$}\boxed{\$}\boxed{\$}\ \$$$
2003

THINK: Prize in 1973   = $6 − $5
               =   Prize in 2003 − $5

How to solve original problem Subtract $56,571 from the 2003 prize, $68,571 − $56,571.

Visualize the simpler problem first.

8. The total amount of prize money given out for a race in a year is called the *total purse*. In 2003, the total purse was $650,000. This was 13 times the amount of the total purse for the 1973 Iditarod. What was the total purse in 1973? ◄MAH 151

Think!

Simpler problem In 2003, the total purse was $6. This was 3 times the amount of the total purse for the race in 1973. What was the total purse in 1973?

Diagram of simpler problem $\boxed{\$\ \$}\ \boxed{\$\ \$}\ \boxed{\$\ \$}$ ←1973
                                 2003

Circle the expression that describes the simpler problem.

   A. 6×3 **B.** $\boxed{6 \div 3}$

Circle the expression that describes the original problem.

   A. $650,000 \times 13$ **B.** $\boxed{\$650,000 \div 13}$

42

Beginning the Lesson

Go over the Example at the top of page 42 with the class. Explain that a simpler problem has the same story but the numbers are smaller or easier to work with. A simpler problem makes diagramming and planning a solution easier. The solution method that works with the simpler numbers will work with the original numbers.

Be sure students understand that there are no rules for deciding which numbers to use in the simpler problem. It can be a good idea to choose a larger number that is a multiple of the smaller number. (6 is a multiple of 3.) That way, if the problem turns out to be one in which the larger number is divided by the smaller number, it can quickly be solved.

Exercises: Getting Started

Have students work independently or in small groups on the exercises on pages 42–43.

Remind students that the pictures they draw on page 43 should be simple. The important point is that they show the math.

9. The longest section on the 2003 trail begins in Cripple and ends in Ruby. This section is 112 miles long. If a musher has just 1.5 miles to go before arriving in Ruby, how far is she from Cripple? ◂ MAH 135

Think!
Simpler problem The total distance from A to B is 10 miles. A musher is between A and B, 2 miles from B. How far is she from A?

Diagram of simpler problem
Sample:

Circle the expression that describes the simpler problem.

A. $10 + 2$ B. $(10 - 2)$

Circle the expression that describes the original problem.

A. $112 + 1.5$ B. $(112 - 1.5)$

10. At one checkpoint, a musher picks up 18 honeyballs for each of his 15 dogs. How many honeyballs does he pick up? ◂ MAH 139

Think!
Simpler problem _Sample answer: A musher picks up 3 honeyballs for each of his 5 dogs._

Diagram of simpler problem
Sample: (XXX) (XXX) (XXX) (XXX) (XXX)

Write the expression that describes the simpler problem. ___5×3___

Circle the expression that describes the original problem.

A. (15×18) B. $18 \div 15$

Did you know?
Honeyballs are a popular dog snack on the trail. They contain lean beef, powdered eggs, and multivitamins. They are high in calories and easy for the dogs to digest.

43

Discussing the Exercises

When going over the exercises, allow time for class discussion.

8–10. Be sure students see how to use what they learn from the simpler problem to decide how to solve the original problem.

9. Ask volunteers to draw their pictures on the board. Discuss the fact that drawings do not need to look alike but must correctly show the math.

10. Be sure students understand that different students will use different numbers in their simpler problems.

Extending the Lesson: Solving the Problems

You may wish to have students use a separate piece of paper to solve the problems.

  8. $50,000

  9. 110.5 miles

10. 270 honeyballs

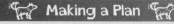
Objectives

Read for understanding.

Choose a plan for solving a problem.

Using Math at Hand

References to handbook items appear with the following exercises.

Exercises 1–2 Item 132 (Subtracting with Regrouping)

Exercise 3 Items 033 and 164 (Fraction of a Set; Subtracting Like Fractions)

Exercise 4 Item 044 (Relating Fractions to Percents)

Having a plan that works is important in problem solving.

Your film will include segments on the planning mushers need to do for the Iditarod. For example, they need to make plans for all the food and equipment they will need for the race. hey need to plan what to bring with them to the starting point and what to send ahead to each of the checkpoints along the way.

When you solve a math problem, try to plan well. Your plan might be simple and have just one step. Or, it may have two or more steps.

In the 1990 race, a musher left the starting line with only one pair of boots, and they were not waterproof. That poor planning forced the musher to drop out of the race.

Sometimes, your plan won't work. You may look at your answer and realize that it just doesn't make sense. Luckily, unlike the musher with the wrong boots, you can go back and try another plan.

Circle the plan that you could use to solve the problem.

1. The route of the Iditarod is not always the same. Unless it's a bad-snow year, a northern route, 1112 miles long, is used in even years and a southern route, 1120 miles long, is used in odd years. This allows more of the people in Alaska to take an active part in helping out with the race. How much longer is the southern route than the northern route? ◄MAH 132

   Plan A
   • Subtract 1112 from 1120.

   Plan B
   • Subtract 1120 from 1112.

   Plan C
   • Add 1220 to 1112.

44

Beginning the Lesson

Use the following question to check students' understanding of the introduction.

* *What mistakes in planning did the musher described in the introduction make?* (The musher should have brought more than one pair of boots and the boots should have been waterproof.)

Exercises: Getting Started

Have students work independently or in small groups on the exercises on pages 44–45.

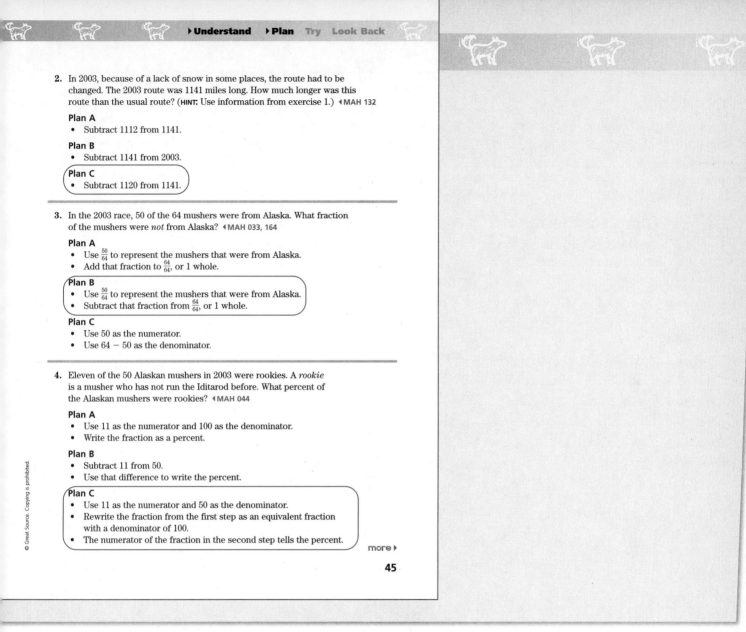

2. In 2003, because of a lack of snow in some places, the route had to be changed. The 2003 route was 1141 miles long. How much longer was this route than the usual route? (HINT: Use information from exercise 1.) ◂MAH 132

Plan A
- Subtract 1112 from 1141.

Plan B
- Subtract 1141 from 2003.

Plan C
- Subtract 1120 from 1141.

3. In the 2003 race, 50 of the 64 mushers were from Alaska. What fraction of the mushers were *not* from Alaska? ◂MAH 033, 164

Plan A
- Use $\frac{50}{64}$ to represent the mushers that were from Alaska.
- Add that fraction to $\frac{64}{64}$, or 1 whole.

Plan B
- Use $\frac{50}{64}$ to represent the mushers that were from Alaska.
- Subtract that fraction from $\frac{64}{64}$, or 1 whole.

Plan C
- Use 50 as the numerator.
- Use $64 - 50$ as the denominator.

4. Eleven of the 50 Alaskan mushers in 2003 were rookies. A *rookie* is a musher who has not run the Iditarod before. What percent of the Alaskan mushers were rookies? ◂MAH 044

Plan A
- Use 11 as the numerator and 100 as the denominator.
- Write the fraction as a percent.

Plan B
- Subtract 11 from 50.
- Use that difference to write the percent.

Plan C
- Use 11 as the numerator and 50 as the denominator.
- Rewrite the fraction from the first step as an equivalent fraction with a denominator of 100.
- The numerator of the fraction in the second step tells the percent.

more ▸

45

Discussing the Exercises

When going over the exercises, allow time for class discussion. For each exercise, ask for a show of hands to determine who chose each plan.

2. *How did you know whether to use 1112 or 1120 in this problem?* (Since 2003 is an odd number, you need to use the length of the southern route, 1120 miles.) *How do you know 2003 is an odd number?* (Possible answer: Its ones digit is odd.)

Extending the Lesson: Solving the Problems

You may wish to have students use a separate piece of paper to solve the problems.

1. 8 miles
2. 21 miles
3. $\frac{14}{64}$ or $\frac{7}{32}$
4. 22%

Objectives

Understand that there may be more than one way to correctly solve a problem.

Use clues to complete plans for solving problems.

Using Math at Hand

References to handbook items appear with the following exercises.

Exercise 5 Items 139 and 132 (Two Ways to Multiply Whole Numbers; Subtracting with Regrouping)

Exercise 7 Items 131–132 (Subtracting with Regrouping)

Exercise 8 Items 176 and 260 (Dividing Mixed Numbers; Mean)

Exercise 9 Items 260 and 151 (Mean; Another Way to Divide)

Sometimes, there's more than one plan that can work.

Circle the plan that you could use to solve the problem. If either plan would work, circle both plans.

5. A musher can buy fleece dog-booties for $0.75 each or stretch dog-booties for $1.25 each. If a musher wants to buy 40 booties for each of his 15 dogs, how much can she save by buying the fleece booties instead of the stretch booties? ◀ MAH 139, 132

Plan A
- To find the total number of booties, multiply 15 by 40.
- To find how much she saves per bootie, subtract $0.75 from $1.25.
- Multiply the answer from the second step by the answer from the first step.

Plan B
- To find the number of booties, multiply 15 by 40.
- To find the cost of all the fleece booties, multiply $0.75 by the answer from the first step.
- To find the cost of all the stretch booties, multiply $1.25 by the answer from the first step.
- Subtract the total cost of the fleece booties from the total cost of the stretch booties.

6. In 2003, the first-place winner, Robert Sorle from Norway, finished the race in 9 days, 15 hours, 47 minutes, and 36 seconds. The last-place finisher, Russell Bybee, finished 5 days, 13 hours, 43 minutes, and 17 seconds later. How long did the last-place finisher take to complete the race?

Plan A
- Add the two times.

Plan B
- Subtract the shorter time from the longer time.

Since 1986, a Red Lantern is hung in Nome at the beginning of the race each year. It burns until the last musher crosses the finish line. The Red Lantern has become a symbol of persistence, an important trait in mushers *and* problem solvers.

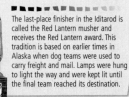

The last-place finisher in the Iditarod is called the Red Lantern musher and receives the Red Lantern award. This tradition is based on earlier times in Alaska when dog teams were used to carry freight and mail. Lamps were hung to light the way and were kept lit until the final team reached its destination.

46

Beginning the Lesson

Direct students' attention to the section at the bottom of page 46 which describes the tradition of calling the musher who comes in last *the Red Lantern musher*.

You may wish to read the introduction on page 47 yourself or have a volunteer read it aloud. If students are not familiar with a relay race, explain how a relay race differs from other races. Explain that one runner runs a certain distance; then the next runner starts where the first runner left off. All runners do not run at the same time.

Exercises: Getting Started

Have students work independently or in small groups on the exercises on pages 46–47.

Discuss the idea that there is often more than one way to correctly solve a problem. Emphasize that one solution method that works may be just as good as different solution methods that work, although sometimes one method is easier to use than the others. When both plans will work, students need to circle both plans.

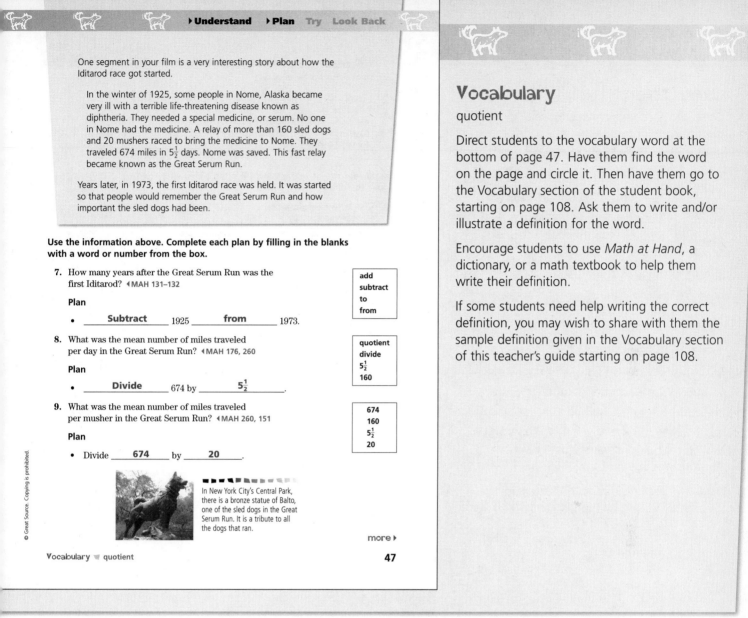

One segment in your film is a very interesting story about how the Iditarod race got started.

In the winter of 1925, some people in Nome, Alaska became very ill with a terrible life-threatening disease known as diphtheria. They needed a special medicine, or serum. No one in Nome had the medicine. A relay of more than 160 sled dogs and 20 mushers raced to bring the medicine to Nome. They traveled 674 miles in $5\frac{1}{2}$ days. Nome was saved. This fast relay became known as the Great Serum Run.

Years later, in 1973, the first Iditarod race was held. It was started so that people would remember the Great Serum Run and how important the sled dogs had been.

Use the information above. Complete each plan by filling in the blanks with a word or number from the box.

7. How many years after the Great Serum Run was the first Iditarod? ◀ MAH 131–132

   Plan

   • ___**Subtract**___ 1925 ___**from**___ 1973.

   | add |
   | subtract |
   | to |
   | from |

8. What was the mean number of miles traveled per day in the Great Serum Run? ◀ MAH 176, 260

   Plan

   • ___**Divide**___ 674 by ___$5\frac{1}{2}$___.

   | quotient |
   | divide |
   | $5\frac{1}{2}$ |
   | 160 |

9. What was the mean number of miles traveled per musher in the Great Serum Run? ◀ MAH 260, 151

   Plan

   • Divide ___**674**___ by ___**20**___.

   | 674 |
   | 160 |
   | $5\frac{1}{2}$ |
   | 20 |

In New York City's Central Park, there is a bronze statue of Balto, one of the sled dogs in the Great Serum Run. It is a tribute to all the dogs that ran.

more ▶

Vocabulary ▾ quotient   47

Vocabulary

quotient

Direct students to the vocabulary word at the bottom of page 47. Have them find the word on the page and circle it. Then have them go to the Vocabulary section of the student book, starting on page 108. Ask them to write and/or illustrate a definition for the word.

Encourage students to use *Math at Hand*, a dictionary, or a math textbook to help them write their definition.

If some students need help writing the correct definition, you may wish to share with them the sample definition given in the Vocabulary section of this teacher's guide starting on page 108.

Discussing the Exercises

When going over the exercises, allow time for class discussion. For exercises 5 and 6, ask for a show of hands to determine who chose each plan, and who chose both plans.

5. Be sure students understand that either plan will work.

Extending the Lesson: Solving the Problems

You may wish to have students use a separate piece of paper to solve the problems.

5. $300

6. 15 days 5 hours 30 minutes 53 seconds (Students may need a reminder that to find the final answer, they need to rewrite 60 min as 1 h, and then 24 h as 1 day.)

7. 48 years

8. $122.\overline{54}$ miles or $122\frac{6}{11}$ miles

9. 33.7 miles or $33\frac{7}{10}$ miles

Objectives

Use clues to complete plans for solving problems.

Read a problem and plan the solution.

Using Math at Hand

References to handbook items appear with the following exercises.

Exercise 10 Item 260 (Mean)

Exercise 11 Item 257 (Range)

Exercise 12 Item 262 (Mode)

Exercise 13 Item 261 (Median)

Exercise 14 Items 139 and 132 (Two Ways to Multiply Whole Numbers; Subtracting with Regrouping)

Exercise 15 Items 139 and 122 (Two Ways to Multiply Whole Numbers; Adding with Regrouping)

Exercise 16 Items 096 and 091 (Rounding Decimals; Dividing by 10, 100, and 1000)

Completing a plan can help you learn to make your own plan.

To plan the race segments of your film, you need to know the real segments of the race. The Iditarod routes are divided into sections with a checkpoint at the end of each section. The table shows the distances in miles for the 22 sections that make up the 2003 route.

Checkpoint	Distance from Previous Check
Anchorage	
Restart in Fairbanks	20 mi
1	53 mi
2	100 mi
3	60 mi
4	115 mi
5	52 mi
6	52 mi
7	42 mi
8	70 mi
9	60 mi
10	18 mi
11	18 mi
12	60 mi
13	70 mi
14	90 mi
15	42 mi
16	48 mi
17	48 mi
18	28 mi
19	18 mi
20	55 mi
Nome	22 mi
total distance:	1141 mi

Use the information in the table. Fill in the blanks with a word or number from the box.

10. What is the mean distance between checkpoints? ◄ MAH 260

add	divide
subtract	2
multiply	22

Plan

• ___Divide___ the total distance by ___22___.

11. What is the range of distances between checkpoints? ◄ MAH 257

greatest	subtract
least	from
add	to

Plan

• Find the greatest distance in the table.

• Find the least distance in the table.

• ___Subtract___ the ___least___ distance ___from___ the ___greatest___ distance.

12. Which distance is the mode? ◄ MAH 262

most
least
twice as

Plan

• Find the distance in the table which occurs ___most___ often.

13. What is the median of the distances? ◄ MAH 261

first	average
last	sum
middle	

Plan

• Write the distances in order from least to greatest.

• The median is the ___average___ of the two ___middle___ numbers.

48   Vocabulary ☞ median ☞ sum

Connecting to the Theme

Each year the Iditarod begins in Anchorage. In recent years this has become a ceremonial start in a location that allows many people to see the start of the race. The mushers and the dogs travel to a given destination; then they are transported to another location, where the race restarts. In 2003, the restart was in Fairbanks. The location of the restart changes according to the amount of snow and other conditions.

Beginning the Lesson

Read the introduction yourself or have a student volunteer read it aloud. Use the following questions to check students' understanding of the introduction.

• *How many sections were in the 2003 race?* (22 sections)

• *What is the total distance of the 2003 race?* (1141 miles)

Exercises: Getting Started

Have students work independently or in small groups on the exercises on pages 48–49.

You and your friends visit a souvenir store. You see these items for sale. The prices include tax.

Husky Pup Toy $9.95   Iditarod Ruler $0.95   Baseball Cap $7.95

Use the information shown above. Write a plan for solving each problem.

14. You buy two baseball caps. How much change do you get from a $20-bill? ◂MAH 139, 132

    Sample answers are provided.

    Plan

    To find the cost of the caps, **multiply $7.95 by 2.**

    Subtract the product from $20.

15. Nathan buys 3 rulers and a book about the Iditarod that costs $5.25. What is the total cost? ◂MAH 139, 122

    Plan

    Multiply $0.95 by 3.

    Add $5.25 to the product.

16. Kathleen buys some husky pups and a baseball cap. The total cost is $47.75. Use estimation to find how many husky pups Kathleen buys. ◂MAH 096, 091

    Plan

    Subtract $8 from $48.

    Divide the difference by 10.

    more ▸

    49

Vocabulary

median   sum

Direct students to the vocabulary words at the bottom of page 48. Have them find the words on the page and circle them. Then have them go to the Vocabulary section of the student book, starting on page 108. Ask them to write and/or illustrate definitions for the words.

Encourage students to use *Math at Hand*, a dictionary, or a math textbook to help them write their definitions.

If some students need help writing correct definitions, you may wish to share with them the sample definitions given in the Vocabulary section of this teacher's guide starting on page 108.

Optional Follow Up

Have students make a stem-and-leaf plot of the data in the table on page 48. (See Item 284 in *Math at Hand*.) Discuss whether the stem-and-leaf plot makes it easier to find the mean, median, mode, and range. (Students should see that the stem-and-leaf plot makes it easier to find the median, mode, and range.)

0	
1	8 8 8
2	0 2 8
3	
4	2 2 8 8
5	2 2 3 5
6	0 0 0
7	0 0
8	
9	0
10	0
11	5

Discussing the Exercises

When going over the exercises, allow time for class discussion.

14–16. Carefully discuss and compare students' plans. You may wish to have students use their plans to write expressions that could be used to solve the problems:

14. $20 - (2 \times \$7.95)$ or $20 - 2 \times \$7.95$

15. $(3 \times \$0.95) + \$5.25$ or $3 \times \$0.95 + \$5.25$

16. $(\$48 - \$8) \div \$10.00$

Extending the Lesson: Solving the Problems

You may wish to have students use a separate piece of paper to solve the problems.

10. $51\frac{9}{22}$ miles

11. 97 miles

12. There are two modes: 18 miles and 60 miles

13. 52 miles

14. $4.10

15. $8.10

16. 4 husky pups

Objective

Read a problem and plan the solution.

Using Math at Hand

References to handbook items appear with the following exercises.

Exercise 18 Items 274 and 033 (Double-Bar Graphs; Fraction of a Set)

Exercise 19 Items 178–179 (Ratios)

Exercise 20 Item 282 (Line Plots)

Exercise 21 Item 113 (Estimating Quotients Using Compatible Numbers)

Exercise 22 Item 322 (Time)

Making a good plan is the key to problem solving.

You meet a 16-year old boy who tells you about the Junior Iditarod. This is a race which is held on the weekend just before the Iditarod race begins. Mushers must be at least 14 years old but not yet 18.

Write a plan for solving each problem.   Sample answers are provided.

17. Your new friend tells you that he was a musher in the 2003 Junior Iditarod race. Nineteen mushers started the race, but one dropped out. Your friend came in fifth. How many mushers finished behind him?

Plan

Subtract 1 from 19.

Subtract 5 from the difference.

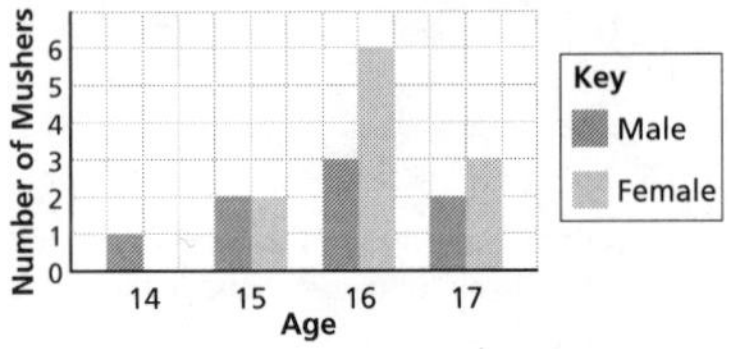

18. This bar graph shows the ages of the mushers who raced in the 2003 Junior Iditarod. What fraction of the mushers were 15 or younger? ◄MAH 274, 033

Age of Mushers in 2003 Junior Iditarod

Key
■ Male
■ Female

Plan

Add the number of 14-year-olds to the number of 15-year-olds.

Use the sum as the numerator.

Find the total number of mushers.

Use the total number of mushers as the denominator.

19. Use the bar graph from exercise 20. What was the ratio of males to females in the 2003 Junior Iditarod? ◄MAH 178–179

Plan

Find the total number of males.

Find the total number of females.

Write a ratio, number of males : number of females.

Beginning the Lesson

Read the introduction yourself or have a student volunteer read it aloud.

Use the following question to check students' understanding of the introduction.

* *Mushers in the Junior Iditarod can be what ages?*
  (14, 15, 16, or 17)

Exercises: Getting Started

Have students work independently or in small groups on the exercises on pages 50–51.

20. The line plot shows the number of dogs on each of the 18 teams that finished the 2003 Junior Iditarod. How many dogs finished the race? ◂MAH 282

Number of Dogs on Each Team 2003 Junior Iditarod Finishers

Plan

For each number of dogs, multiply the number of Xs by that number.

Add the 5 products.

21. A 17-year old musher, came in first. She finished the 160-mile race in about $11\frac{1}{2}$ hours. About what was her average speed in miles per hour? ◂MAH 113

Plan

Divide 160 miles by $11\frac{1}{2}$ hours.

The answer will be in miles per hour.

22. The musher who came in next-to-last finished the race in 21 hours 8 minutes. The Red Lantern musher (the last-place finisher) finished the race $\frac{1}{2}$ hour after that. What was the Red Lantern musher's time? ◂MAH 322

Plan

Rewrite $\frac{1}{2}$ hour as 30 minutes.

Add 30 minutes to 21 hours 8 minutes.

Your trip to Alaska to learn about the Iditarod is now over. It's time to head back home.

When you're at home working on a math problem and you find yourself stumped, think about the Red Lantern musher. Stick it out. If your first plan for solving a problem doesn't work, try another plan. Take a break if you need to, but don't give up!

51

Optional Follow Up

Write the following table (without the numbers) on the chalkboard. Have students copy the table and put in numbers so that the table shows the same information as the bar graph.

Age Of Mushers in 2003 Junior Iditarod

Age	Males	Females
14	1	0
15	2	2
16	3	6
17	2	3

Discussing the Exercises

When going over the exercises, allow time for class discussion. Carefully discuss and compare students' plans for each problem.

Extending the Lesson: Solving the Problems

You may wish to have students use a separate piece of paper to solve the problems.

17. 13 mushers
18. $\frac{5}{19}$
19. 8 to 11
20. 155 dogs
21. about 14 mph
22. 21 hours 38 minutes

Assessment

Two forms of the chapter test are available: the test on these two student pages and the test provided on the copymasters on pages 126–127 of this teacher's guide.

You can use these two forms of the test in the way that works best for you.

- Use one test as a pretest and the other as a posttest.
- Use one test as a practice test and one for assessment.
- Use one test as assessment and the other for a make-up test for students who were absent or who did poorly and need a chance to try again.

Fill in the circle with the letter of the correct answer.

1. Kerri knitted 8 pairs of gloves. To find the number of gloves she knitted, which picture could you use?

   (A)   (B)   (C)

2. One third of the 18 students on the sixth-grade cross-country team are boys. Which picture could you use to find the number of boys on the sixth-grade cross-country team?

   (A)   (B)   (C)

3. Glen is 4 feet tall. His older brother Ned is $1\frac{1}{2}$ times as tall. Which picture could you use to find Ned's height?

   (A)   (B)

4. Charlene turned 11 on March 12, 2003. Which expression would you use to find the year Charlene was born?

   (A) $2003 + 11$ (B) $2003 - 11$ (C) $2003 + 12$ (D) $2003 - 12$

5. Mr. Edwards drove 122 miles in 3 hours. Which expression would you use to find his average speed in miles per hour?

   (A) $122 + 3$ (B) $122 - 3$ (C) 122×3 (D) $122 \div 3$

6. There are 25 students in Mrs. LeFave's class. Thirteen of them are boys. Which of the following tells how to find the fraction of students in Mrs. LeFave's class that are girls?

   (A) **Plan A**
   - Subtract 13 from 25 and use that difference as the numerator.
   - Use 25 as the denominator.

   (B) **Plan B**
   - Use 13 as the numerator and 25 as the denominator.

52

Name _____ Date _____

Fill in the circle with the letter of the correct answer.

1. Mrs. Chang bought 3 bags of apples. Each bag had 8 apples. To find the total number of apples, which picture could you use?

   (A)   (B)   (C)

2. One fifth of the 20 students on the middle school track team are boys. Which picture could you use to find the number of boys on the middle school track team?

   (A)   (B)   (C) ×××⊗××××××××××××××

3. Carly ran 4 miles. Her older sister Kerri ran $2\frac{1}{2}$ times as far. Which picture could you use to find the distance Kerri ran?

   (A)   (B)

4. Charlene turned 14 on September 13, 2003. Which expression would you use to find the year Charlene was born?

   (A) $2003 + 14$ (B) $2003 - 14$ (C) $2003 + 13$ (D) $2003 - 13$

5. Mr. Randall drove 155 miles in 5 hours. Which expression would you use to find his average speed in miles per hour?

   (A) $155 + 5$ (B) $155 - 5$ (C) 155×5 (D) $155 \div 5$

6. There are 25 students in Mr. Carlson's class. Twelve of them are girls. Which of the following tells how to find the fraction of students in Mr. Carlson's class that are boys?

   (A) **Plan A**
   - Subtract 12 from 25.
   - Use that difference as the numerator.
   - Use 25 as the denominator.

   (B) **Plan B**
   - Use 12 as the numerator and 25 as the denominator.

126

Name _____ Date _____

Choose the letter of the best answer, then write why you made that choice.

7. Harold took 4 spelling tests. His scores were 90, 82, 85, 80, and 85. Which plan tells how to find Harold's mean score?

   (A) **Plan A**
   - Add the scores. _____
   - Divide the sum by 5. _____

   (B) **Plan B**
   - Order the scores least to greatest. _____
   - Use the middle score. _____

Write the plan you would use to answer the question.

8. Out of the 50 students in the band, 3 missed the concert. How would you find the percent of students in the band that missed the concert?

   Plan

   _____
   _____
   _____
   _____

Write a math word problem that could be solved by using this plan.

9. Plan
   - Multiply $4.50 by 3.
   - Subtract the product from $20.00.

   _____
   _____
   _____

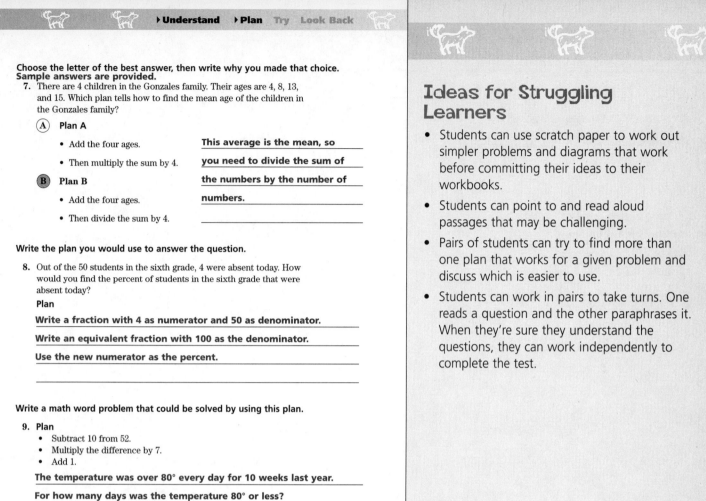

Choose the letter of the best answer, then write why you made that choice. Sample answers are provided.

7. There are 4 children in the Gonzales family. Their ages are 4, 8, 13, and 15. Which plan tells how to find the mean age of the children in the Gonzales family?

   (A) **Plan A**

   • Add the four ages.

   • Then multiply the sum by 4.

   (B) **Plan B**

   • Add the four ages.

   • Then divide the sum by 4.

   This average is the mean, so you need to divide the sum of the numbers by the number of numbers.

Write the plan you would use to answer the question.

8. Out of the 50 students in the sixth grade, 4 were absent today. How would you find the percent of students in the sixth grade that were absent today?

   Plan

   Write a fraction with 4 as numerator and 50 as denominator.

   Write an equivalent fraction with 100 as the denominator.

   Use the new numerator as the percent.

Write a math word problem that could be solved by using this plan.

9. **Plan**
   • Subtract 10 from 52.
   • Multiply the difference by 7.
   • Add 1.

   The temperature was over 80° every day for 10 weeks last year.

   For how many days was the temperature 80° or less?

53

Ideas for Struggling Learners

• Students can use scratch paper to work out simpler problems and diagrams that work before committing their ideas to their workbooks.

• Students can point to and read aloud passages that may be challenging.

• Pairs of students can try to find more than one plan that works for a given problem and discuss which is easier to use.

• Students can work in pairs to take turns. One reads a question and the other paraphrases it. When they're sure they understand the questions, they can work independently to complete the test.

Answers for Alternate Form Test

1. A	4. B
2. B	5. D
3. B	6. A

7. A; Possible explanation: To find the mean, you need to divide the sum of the scores by the number of scores. Plan B finds the median.

8. Sample answer: Write a fraction with 3 as numerator and 50 as denominator. Write an equivalent fraction with 100 as the denominator. Use the numerator as the percent.

9. Sample answer: I gave the cashier a $20-bill to pay for 3 pairs of socks that cost $4.50 each. What change will I get?

Chapter 4

JOURNEY TO MARS

CARRYING OUT THE PLAN

Using Pages 54–55

Chapter 4

JOURNEY TO MARS

CARRYING OUT THE PLAN

OUTER LOOPS

THE BREAKFAST OF SPACE EXPLORERS

Enter our contest for a free round-trip on the first commercial flight to Mars. Travel in a space shuttle and visit a space station.

To enter: In 25 words or less, tell why you would like to win this trip to Mars. Send what you write and the top from this box of Outer Loops to us.

54

Guiding the Reading

Students should read these two pages independently. Use the copymaster on page 119 of this book to help guide their reading. Be sure students understand that this is not a real contest.

Connecting to the Theme

These are optional ideas for connecting to the theme of space exploration as you do this chapter.

- Have the students pretend they are on a journey to Mars or one of the other planets. Have them write a letter home telling about their journey.

- Have your students work in small groups to design a habitat for one of the planets. You might want to have them look at the *Explore the Planet Mars Simulation* on the Internet to see one example of a habitat before they do this project.

- Have students work in small groups to create a report about an aspect of space exploration. They might write about a planet, a particular space mission, an astronaut, etc.

In this chapter, you'll learn about early space travel and about space travel today. You'll find out how Mars and Earth are alike and how they are different. You'll then be able to decide whether you'd like to travel to Mars. A trip like that would need a lot of planning. In this chapter you'll be making plans to solve word problems. You'll also be carrying out those plans to solve the problems. You'll practice using the second and third steps of the four-step problem-solving method: **Plan** and **Try**.

▼ Two Mars Rovers were launched in mid-2003, the first on June 10 and the second on July 7.

▲ In the 1600s Galileo Galilei became the first person to see Mars through a telescope.

▼ A map of Mars.

Acidalia
Ceraunius   Planitia   Utopia
Tholus   Planitia
Olympus
Mons   Syrtis   Elysium
                    Tharsis   Major   Planitia
        Arsai   Terra   Apollinaris
        Mons   Meridiani   Patera
              Valles Marineris
Gorgonum
Chaos   Noachis   Hellas   Terra
        Sirenum   Argyre   Terra   Planitia Cimmeria
        Fossae   Planitia

▲ Mars is called the red planet because it looks red in the night sky.

55

Sample Answers for Reading Guide

1. Mars
2. in a space shuttle
3. I must write in 25 words or less why I would like to win the trip.
4. It looks red in the night sky.
5. in the 1600s
6. Gailileo Galilei
7. Olympus Mons
8. June 10; July 7
9. Plan and Try

Chapter 4   Reading Guide for Pages 54–55

Name _____ Date _____

1. What planet will the winner of the contest visit? _____

2. How will the winner of the contest travel?
   _____

3. What do you need to do to enter the contest?
   _____

4. Why is Mars called the red planet?
   _____

5. When was Mars first seen through a telescope?
   _____

6. Who was the first person to see Mars through a telescope?
   _____

7. The largest volcano in the solar system is on Mars. Use the map and the letter clues to find its name.
   ___ ___ ___ M ___ U ___ ___ ___ O ___

8. Two Mars Rovers were launched in mid-2003. What were the dates?
   _____

9. Which two problem-solving steps will you practice in Chapter 4?
   _____

119

Bibliography

Caprara, Giovanni. *Living in Space*. Buffalo, New York: Firefly Books, 2000.

Furniss, Tim. *Atlas of Space Exploration*. Milwaukee, Gareth Stevens Publishing, 1999.

Graham, Ian. *The Best Book of Spaceships*. New York: Kingfisher, 1998

Spangenburg, Ray and Kit Moser. *The History of NASA*. Danbury, Connecticut: Franklin Watts, 2000.

Websites

Mars Exploration
http://mars.jpl.nasa.gov/index.html
   Information about Mars and games and activities.

Mars: Extreme Planet
http://mars.jpl.nasa.gov/extreme/index.html
   Description of the environment on Mars.

Explore the Planet Mars Simulation
http://www.exploremarsnow.org/
   A simulation of a possible Mars habitat.

Objectives

Read to find information relevant to a problem.

Write and carry out a plan to solve a problem.

Using Math at Hand

References to handbook items appear with the following exercises.

Exercise 1 Item 033 (Fraction of a Set)

Exercise 2 Items 033 and 044 (Fraction of a Set; Relating Fractions to Percent)

Exercise 3 Item 287 (Notation and Calculating Probability)

Connecting to the Theme

After students have corrected their Space Quizzes, you may wish to challenge them to name the important space-related events that happened in 1957, 1969, and 1998 (the incorrect choices for question 2.)

- **1957:** Soviets launch *Sputnik 1;* Laika, a dog aboard *Sputnik 2,* is the first animal in space.
- **1969:** First men on moon
- **1998:** The first part of the International Space Station is launched.

After you write a plan, it is important to know how to carry out that plan.

Here's a short quiz to find out how much you may already know about early space travel.

Take the quiz and see how many questions you can answer correctly.

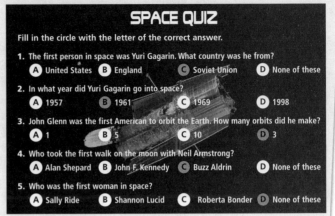

SPACE QUIZ

Fill in the circle with the letter of the correct answer.

1. The first person in space was Yuri Gagarin. What country was he from?
A United States   **B** England   **C** Soviet Union   **D** None of these

2. In what year did Yuri Gagarin go into space?
A 1957   **B** 1961   **C** 1969   **D** 1998

3. John Glenn was the first American to orbit the Earth. How many orbits did he make?
A 1   **B** 5   **C** 10   **D** 3

4. Who took the first walk on the moon with Neil Armstrong?
A Alan Shepard   **B** John F. Kennedy   **C** Buzz Aldrin   **D** None of these

5. Who was the first woman in space?
A Sally Ride   **B** Shannon Lucid   **C** Roberta Bonder   **D** None of these

Use the quiz above to solve the problems. The first is done for you.

1. Suppose Manuel answered 2 questions incorrectly. What fraction of the questions did he answer correctly? ◄MAH 033

Plan Fill in the blanks.

- First, write the fraction of the questions Manuel answered *incorrectly.*

  Use ___2___ as the numerator and 5 as the denominator.

- Subtract that fraction from ___$\frac{5}{5}$ or 1___ .

Try Circle the equation that fits the plan.

A. $\left(\frac{5}{5} - \frac{2}{5} = \frac{3}{5}\right)$ B. $\frac{5}{5} - \frac{3}{5} = \frac{2}{5}$ C. $\frac{5}{5} - \frac{1}{5} = \frac{4}{5}$

Complete the answer. Manuel answered ___$\frac{3}{5}$___ of the questions correctly.

56

Then challenge students to identify the men and woman used as incorrect responses for exercises 4 and 5.

- **Alan Shepard** was the first American in space.
- **John F. Kennedy** was the president of the U.S. when Alan Shepard went into space.
- **Sally Ride** was the first *American* woman in space.
- In 1996, **Shannon Lucid** spent more than 6 months on the Russian Space Station *Mir*.
- **Roberta Bonder** was the first Canadian woman in space.
- Note: The first woman in space was **Valentina Tereshkova** from the USSR (June 16, 1963)

Beginning the Lesson

Have each student take the Space Quiz on page 56. Students can correct their quizzes (answers are on student page 69) anytime before they begin exercises 4–6. When they have finished correcting them, you may wish to share the information in *Connecting to the Theme*.

Exercises: Getting Started

Have students work independently or in small groups on the exercises on pages 56–57. Exercise 1 has been done and can serve as a sample.

2. Suppose Jenny answered 4 questions correctly. What percent of the questions did Jenny answer correctly? ◂ MAH 033, 044

Plan Fill in the blanks.

THINK: Write the fraction of the questions Jenny answered correctly.

Use ____4____ as the numerator and 5 as the denominator.

- Rewrite the fraction as an equivalent fraction with a denominator of ____100____.

- The ____numerator____ of the new fraction tells the percent.

Try Circle the solution that fits the plan.

A. $\frac{1}{5} = \frac{20}{100}$
   $= 20\%$

B. $\frac{4}{5} = \frac{8}{10}$
   $= 8\%$

C. $\frac{4}{5} = \frac{80}{100}$
   $= 80\%$

Complete the answer. Jenny answered ____80%____ of the questions correctly.

3. Suppose Sam has no idea about the answer to question 5. He makes a guess. What is the probability that his guess is correct? ◂ MAH 287

Plan Fill in the blanks.

THINK: Write the probability as a fraction.

- Use the number of favorable outcomes as the ____numerator____.

- Use the number of possible outcomes as the ____denominator____.

Try Circle the solution that fits the plan.

A. $\frac{1 \leftarrow \text{favorable}}{4 \leftarrow \text{possible}}$

B. $\frac{1 \leftarrow \text{favorable}}{5 \leftarrow \text{possible}}$

C. $\frac{4 \leftarrow \text{favorable}}{1 \leftarrow \text{possible}}$

Complete the answer. The probability that Sam's guess is correct is ____$\frac{1}{4}$____.

Look on page 69 for the answers to the quiz. Correct your quiz. Then use plans like those for exercises 1–2 to answer questions 5–6. **Answers will vary.**

4. How many questions did you answer correctly? _____

5. What fraction of the questions did you answer correctly? _____

6. What percent of the questions did you answer correctly? _____

more ▸

Vocabulary ▾ probability ▾ outcome ▾ favorable outcome

57

Vocabulary

favorable outcome

outcome

probability

Direct students to the vocabulary words at the bottom of page 57. Have them find each word on the page and circle it. Then have them go to the Vocabulary section of the student book, starting on page 108. Ask them to write and/or illustrate a definition for the word.

Encourage them to use *Math at Hand*, a dictionary, or a math textbook to help them write their definition.

If some students need help writing the correct definitions, you may wish to share with them the sample definitions given in this teacher's guide starting on page 108.

Optional Follow Up

Survey the class to determine the percent of quiz questions each student answered correctly. Make a tally chart to show the results. Have students make a bar graph or a circle graph to display the results. Discuss why a line graph would not be appropriate to show this data. (A line graph shows change over time.)

Discussing the Exercises

When going over the exercises, allow time for class discussion.

1. *What fraction of the questions did Manuel answer incorrectly?* $\left(\frac{2}{5}\right)$

2. *What percent of the questions did Jenny answer incorrectly?* (20%)

3. *What is the probability that Sam's guess is incorrect?* $\left(\frac{3}{4}\right)$

Objectives

Read critically to discover relationships between numbers in a problem.

Make a plan based on relationships between numbers in a problem.

Using Math at Hand

References to handbook items appear with the following exercises.

Exercise 8 Items 324 and 325 (Elapsed Time; Time Zones)

Exercise 9 Item 168 (Multiplying a Whole Number by a Fraction)

Exercise 10 Item 486 (The Customary System: Time)

When carrying out your plan, it's important to check all the details.

Follow the steps to solve the problems.

7. On April 12, 1961 Yuri Gagarin, a Soviet, became the first person in space. Just 23 days later, Alan Shepard became the first American in space. What was the date of Alan Shepard's flight?

Plan Fill in the blanks.

THINK: There are ____30____ days in April.

- Find how many of the 23 days were in April (after ____April 12____).

- Subtract that number from ____23____.

- The difference will tell how many of the 23 days were in ____May____.

Try Circle the solution that fits the plan.

A. (30 − 12 = 18, so 18 days in April   23 − 18 = 5, so 5 days in May)

B. 31 − 12 = 19, so 19 days in April   23 − 19 = 4, so 4 days in May

Complete the answer. Alan Shepard's flight was on ____May 5, 1961____.

---

8. John Glenn was the first American in orbit. That flight took 4 hours and 55 minutes. The launch occurred at 9:47 A.M. Eastern Standard Time (EST). At what time (EST) did he land? ◀ MAH 324, 325

Plan Fill in the blanks.

THINK: 4 hours 55 minutes is ____5____ minutes less than 5 hours.

- Count on ____5____ hours from ____9:47 A.M.____

- Count back ____5____ minutes.

Try Circle the solution that fits the plan.

A. (9:47 A.M. → 10:47 A.M. → 11:47 A.M. → 12:47 P.M. → 1:47 P.M. → 2:47 P.M. → 2:42 P.M.)

B. 9:47 A.M. → 10:47 A.M. → 11:47 A.M. → 11:42 P.M.

C. 9:47 A.M. → 10:47 A.M. → 11:47 A.M. → 12:47 P.M. → 1:47 P.M. → 2:47 P.M. → 2:52 P.M.

Complete the answer. John Glenn landed at ____2:42 P.M.____

58   Vocabulary ◦ hour (h) ◦ minute (min)

Exercises: Getting Started

Have students work independently or in small groups on the exercises on pages 58–59.

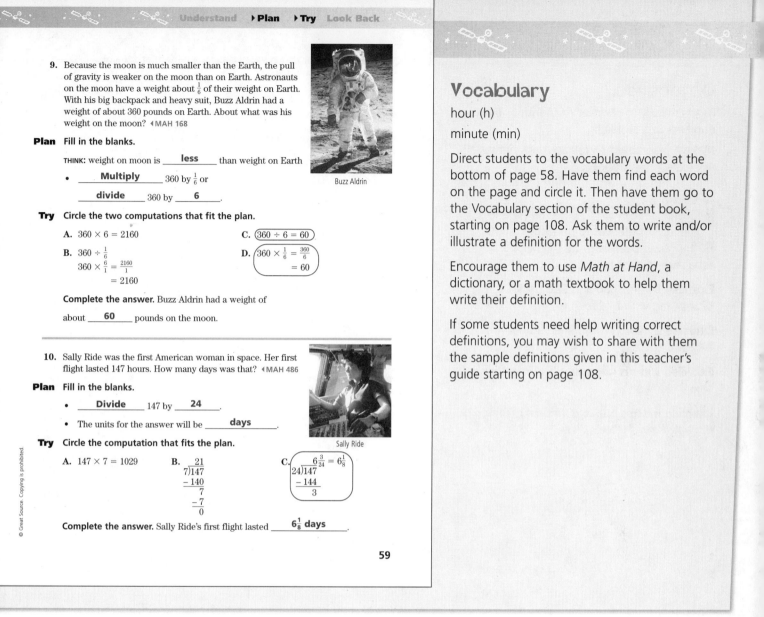

9. Because the moon is much smaller than the Earth, the pull of gravity is weaker on the moon than on Earth. Astronauts on the moon have a weight about $\frac{1}{6}$ of their weight on Earth. With his big backpack and heavy suit, Buzz Aldrin had a weight of about 360 pounds on Earth. About what was his weight on the moon? ◂MAH 168

Buzz Aldrin

Plan Fill in the blanks.

THINK: weight on moon is ____**less**____ than weight on Earth

• ____**Multiply**____ 360 by $\frac{1}{6}$ or

____**divide**____ 360 by ____**6**____.

Try Circle the two computations that fit the plan.

A. $360 \times 6 = 2160$

B. $360 \div \frac{1}{6}$
$360 \times \frac{6}{1} = \frac{2160}{1}$
$= 2160$

C. $\boxed{360 \div 6 = 60}$

D. $\boxed{360 \times \frac{1}{6} = \frac{360}{6}}$
$\boxed{= 60}$

Complete the answer. Buzz Aldrin had a weight of about ____**60**____ pounds on the moon.

10. Sally Ride was the first American woman in space. Her first flight lasted 147 hours. How many days was that? ◂MAH 486

Plan Fill in the blanks.

• ____**Divide**____ 147 by ____**24**____.

• The units for the answer will be ____**days**____.

Try Circle the computation that fits the plan.

Sally Ride

A. $147 \times 7 = 1029$

B. $\begin{array}{r} 21 \\ 7\overline{)147} \\ -140 \\ \hline 7 \\ -7 \\ \hline 0 \end{array}$

C. $\boxed{\begin{array}{r} 6\frac{3}{24} = 6\frac{1}{8} \\ 24\overline{)147} \\ -144 \\ \hline 3 \end{array}}$

Complete the answer. Sally Ride's first flight lasted ____$6\frac{1}{8}$ **days**____.

Vocabulary

hour (h)

minute (min)

Direct students to the vocabulary words at the bottom of page 58. Have them find each word on the page and circle it. Then have them go to the Vocabulary section of the student book, starting on page 108. Ask them to write and/or illustrate a definition for the words.

Encourage them to use *Math at Hand*, a dictionary, or a math textbook to help them write their definition.

If some students need help writing correct definitions, you may wish to share with them the sample definitions given in this teacher's guide starting on page 108.

Discussing the Exercises

When going over the exercises, allow time for class discussion.

7. *How do you remember that there are only 30 days in April?* (Possible answer: I remember the rhyme: Thirty days hath September, April, June, and November.) Some students may have difficulty understanding why April 30 is 18 days after April 12. Explain that April 13 is one day after April 12 $(13 - 12 = 1)$, April 15 is 3 days after April 12 $(15 - 12 = 3)$, so April 30 is 18 days after April 12 $(30 - 12 = 18)$

8. *How do you know that 4 hours 55 minutes is 5 minutes less than 5 hours?* (There are 60 minutes in an hour. Five hours is the same as 4 hours 60 minutes.)

9. *Why can either computation C or computation D give the correct answer?* (Dividing by 6 gives the same result as multiplying by $\frac{1}{6}$. Dividing by a number is the same as multiplying by the reciprocal of that number.)

10. *How many hours are in a day?* (24) *How did you decide whether to multiply or divide 147 by 24?* (Possible answer: The number of days had to be less than the number of hours.)

Discuss alternative plans that could be used to solve problems 7 and 8. For these, students might use standard classroom items—calendars and clocks—as models.

Objectives

Read critically to discover relationships between numbers in a problem.

Make a plan based on relationships between numbers in a problem.

Using Math at Hand

References to handbook items appear with the following exercises.

Exercise 1 Items 486 and 086 (Time; Multiplying with Multiples of 10)

Exercise 2 Item 120 (Adding without Regrouping)

Exercise 3 Items 486 and 176 (Time; Dividing Mixed Numbers)

Exercise 4 Items 486 and 142–143 (Time; Multiplying with Decimals)

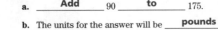
Using a Plan to Solve a Problem

Remember that sometimes problems have too little or too much information.

In 1981, the first space shuttle took off. The shuttle is the only space ship that takes off like a rocket and lands like a plane.

Follow the steps to solve the problems. **Sample answers are provided.**

1. A space shuttle can travel 5 miles per second. How many miles per hour is that? ◄MAH 486, 086

Plan Fill in the blanks.

a. Find the number of seconds in an hour. Multiply ___60___ by ___60___.

b. Multiply the number of seconds in an hour by ___5___.

c. The units for the answer will be ___miles per hour___.

Try Show your work. Write your answer as a complete sentence.
seconds per hour: 60 × 60 = 3600
miles per hour: 3600 × 5 = 18,000
A space shuttle can travel 18,000 miles per hour.

2. During take off and landing, shuttle astronauts wear launch/entry suits (LES). These 90-pound suits protect them from changes in temperature and gravity. If an astronaut weighs 175 pounds on Earth, what will be his Earth-weight when wearing the LES? ◄MAH 120

Plan Fill in the blanks.

a. ___Add___ 90 ___to___ 175.

b. The units for the answer will be ___pounds___.

Try Show your work. Write your answer as a complete sentence.

$$\begin{array}{r} 175 \\ + 90 \\ \hline 265 \end{array}$$

The astronaut will weigh

265 pounds in his LES.

It is hard to move fast when you are wearing an LES. It contains many parts including a helmet, a parachute, a flotation device, and boots.

60   Vocabulary ▾ weight

Exercises: Getting Started

Have students work independently or in small groups on the exercises on pages 60–61. Point out that they will need to show their work in the space provided and write the answer as a complete sentence.

3. During one day, an astronaut on a space shuttle will see a sunset every $1\frac{1}{2}$ hours. How many sunsets per day is that? ◂MAH 486, 176

Plan Fill in the blanks.

- _____Divide_____ 24 _____by_____ $1\frac{1}{2}$.

Try Show your work. Write your answer as a complete sentence.

$24 \div 1\frac{1}{2} \rightarrow 24 \div \frac{3}{2} \rightarrow 24 \times \frac{2}{3}$

$\frac{\cancel{24}^{8}}{1} \times \frac{2}{\cancel{3}_{1}} = 16$

The astronaut will see 16 sunsets

per day.

> **D**id you know?
> Before the space shuttle, astronauts rode in a small capsule perched on the tip of a giant rocket. These early spaceships could fly only once. The shuttle and its rocket boosters can be used many times.

---

4. In 1990, the Hubble Space Telescope (HST) was put into orbit 384 miles above the Earth. Even from that distance, it can photograph a coin on the ground! The HST is 562 inches long, 196 inches across and, on Earth, weighs 12.5 tons. How many pounds does the HST weigh on Earth? ◂MAH 486, 142–143

Plan Fill in the blanks.

THINK: number of _____pounds_____ = 2000 × number of _____tons_____

- _____Multiply_____ 12.5 by _____2000_____.

- The units for the answer will be _____pounds_____.

Try Show your work. Write your answer as a complete sentence.

$$\begin{array}{r} 2000 \\ \times\ 12.5 \\ \hline 25{,}000.0 \end{array}$$

The HST weighs 25,000 pounds.

© Great Source. Copying is prohibited.

Vocabulary

weight

Direct students to the vocabulary word at the bottom of page 60. Have them find the word on the page and circle it. Then have them go to the Vocabulary section of the student book, starting on page 108. Ask them to write and/or illustrate a definition for the word.

Encourage them to use *Math at Hand*, a dictionary, or a math textbook to help them write their definition.

If some students need help writing the correct definition, you may wish to share with them the sample definition given in this teacher's guide starting on page 108.

Discussing the Exercises

When going over the exercises, allow time for class discussion.

1. *How many seconds are in an hour?* (60 × 60 or 3600 seconds) *Will the shuttle travel more miles in a second or in an hour?* (in an hour) *Should you multiply or divide?* (multiply)

3. *Where does the 24 come from?* (the number of hours in a day)

4. *Which numbers from the problem are not needed to solve the problem?* (1990, 384, 562, 196) *What information do you need to know to solve this problem?* (the number of pounds in a ton)

© Great Source. Copying is prohibited.

Objectives

Read for understanding.

Plan and carry out a solution to a problem.

Using Math at Hand

References to handbook items appear with the following exercises.

Exercise 1 Items 310 and 137–141 (Volume of Rectangular Prisms; Multiplying with Whole Numbers)

Exercise 2 Items 096 and 112–113 (Rounding Decimals; Estimating Quotients)

Exercise 3 Items 136 and 486 (Multiplication; Time)

Exercise 4 Item 327 (Changing from One Unit to Another)

A good plan is the key to solving a problem.

Follow the steps to solve each problem.   Sample answers are provided.

1. Astronauts practice space walking in the world's largest indoor pool in Houston. They wear a suit that does not let them sink or float. This lets them experience weightlessness. The pool is 40 feet deep, 102 feet wide and 202 feet long. What is the volume of the pool? ◂MAH 310, 137–141

Plan • Multiply length times width times depth.

• The answer will be in cubic feet.

Try Show your work. Write your answer as a complete sentence.

$202 \times 102 \times 40 = 824,160$

The volume of the pool is 824,160 cubic feet.

2. A cubic-foot container can hold 7.481 gallons. Round and use compatible numbers to estimate the number of gallons of water needed to fill the pool in Houston. (**HINT**: Use information from problem 1.) ◂MAH 096, 112–113

Plan • Round 7.481 to 7.

• Find a number near 824,160 that's compatible with 7.

• Divide the compatible numbers.

Try Show your work. Write your answer as a complete sentence. **Estimates will vary.**

$840,000 \div 7 = 120,000$

The pool in Houston will hold about 120,000 gallons of water.

Astronauts in space don't feel the force of Earth's gravity.

Vocabulary ◂ round a number ◂ compatible number

Exercises: Getting Started

Have students work independently or in small groups on the exercises on pages 62–63.

Point out that any plan that works is acceptable. There is not always just one plan to solve a problem. Also, the same plan can usually be worded in several different ways.

A space station is a large laboratory orbiting Earth. Astronauts live and work there. They do research to learn what they need to know to further explore Mars and the rest of our solar system. Space stations are built on Earth and assembled in space.

3. Shannon Lucid, a U. S. astronaut, spent 26 weeks 6 days on the Russian space station *Mir*. Her journey began on March 22, 1996. How many days did she spend on *Mir*? ◂MAH 136, 486

Plan • **Find the number of days in 26 weeks: Multiply 26 by 7.**

• **Add 6 to that product.**

Try Show your work. Write your answer as a complete sentence.

$$\begin{array}{r} 26 \\ \times\ 7 \\ \hline 182 \end{array} \qquad \begin{array}{r} 182 \\ +\ 6 \\ \hline 188 \end{array}$$

Shannon Lucid spent 188 days on Mir.

4. In 1998, scientists started building the *International Space Station* (ISS). People from 16 countries have been working on it. When it is completed, the ISS will have a length of 356 feet and a width of 290 feet. A football field is 120 yards long and $53\frac{1}{3}$ yards wide. Could the completed ISS fit on a football field? ◂MAH 327

International Space Station

Plan • **Change 120 yards and $53\frac{1}{3}$ yards**

to feet: Multiply by 3.

• **Compare length and width in feet.**

Try Show your work. Use complete sentences to write and explain your answer.

$120 \times 3 = 360$ $53\frac{1}{3} \times 3 = 160$
$360 > 356$ $160 < 290$

No. The ISS is too wide to fit on a football field.

more ▸

Vocabulary

compatible number	week
round a number	yard (yd)

Direct students to the vocabulary words at the bottom of each page. Have them find the words on the page and circle them. Then have them go to the Vocabulary section of the student book, starting on page 108. Ask them to write and/or illustrate a definition for each word.

Encourage them to use *Math at Hand*, a dictionary, or a math textbook to help them write their definition.

If some students need help writing correct definitions, you may wish to share with them the sample definitions given in this teacher's guide starting on page 108.

Optional Follow Up

Have students look back at exercise 3. Have them calculate the date Shannon Lucid returned to Earth. (September 26, 1996)

Discussing the Exercises

When going over the exercises, allow time for class discussion.

1. *What label do we use for the answer?* (cubic feet) *What is a cubic foot?* (the amount of space taken up by a cube 1 foot long, 1 foot wide, and 1 foot high)

2. Have several students share the compatible numbers they used to make their estimate. Be sure they realize that there is not just one set of compatible numbers. While most students will use $840,000 \div 7$, another good choice would be $800,000 \div 8$.

4. Help students to see that finding the area of the space station and finding the area of the football field are not what are needed in order to solve the problem. It is necessary to convert the length and width of the stadium to feet, or the length and width of the space station to yards, and compare the lengths and the widths. Comparing the areas would not be sufficient since the problem asks whether the space station could *fit* in the football field, and in order to do that, it would need to have a length less than the field's length and a width less than the field's width. Having a smaller area would be necessary but not sufficient.

Objectives

Read for understanding.

Plan and carry out a solution to a problem.

Using Math at Hand

References to handbook items appear with the following exercises.

Exercise 5 Items 142–143 (Multiplying with Decimals)

Exercise 6 Item 085–086 (Multiplying by 10, 100, and 1,000; Multiplying with Multiples of 10)

Exercise 7 Items 276 and 168 (Circle Graphs; Multiplying a Whole Number by a Fraction)

Exercise 8 Item 120 (Adding without Regrouping)

If your plan gives you an answer that doesn't make sense, try a new plan.

Follow the steps to solve the problems.   Sample answers are provided.

5. Most of an astronaut's food is dried, because dried food is light and doesn't take up much room. Astronauts eat dried meat, dried fruit, and dried soup. If an astronaut needs 1.5 pounds of dried food per day, how much dried food does she need for the month of March? ◀MAH 142–143

Plan • **Multiply 1.5 by 31.**

• **The answer will be in pounds.**

Try Show your work. Write your answer as a complete sentence.

$$31 \times 1.5 = 46.5$$

She will need 46.5 pounds of food for March.

---

6. The average American uses about 160 gallons of water per day. Only 8 gallons per day is allowed for each person at the space station. How much water per day is allowed for a 5-person crew for 10 days? ◀MAH 085–086

Did you know?
At the space station there is a waterless toilet, food is warmed by dry heat, and water is recycled. The methods we develop to conserve water on the space station will help us conserve water on Earth and, someday, on a trip to Mars.

Plan • **Multiply 8 by 5 to get gallons per day.**

• **Multiply the product by 10 to get gallons for 10 days.**

Try Show your work. Write your answer as a complete sentence.

$$8 \times 5 = 40$$
$$40 \times 10 = 400$$

A 5-person crew will be allowed 400 gallons of water for 10 days.

64

Exercises: Getting Started

Have students work independently or in small groups on the exercises on pages 64–65.

7. The circle graph shows how astronauts on the space station spend each 24-hour day. How many hours per day does an astronaut work? ◂MAH 276, 168

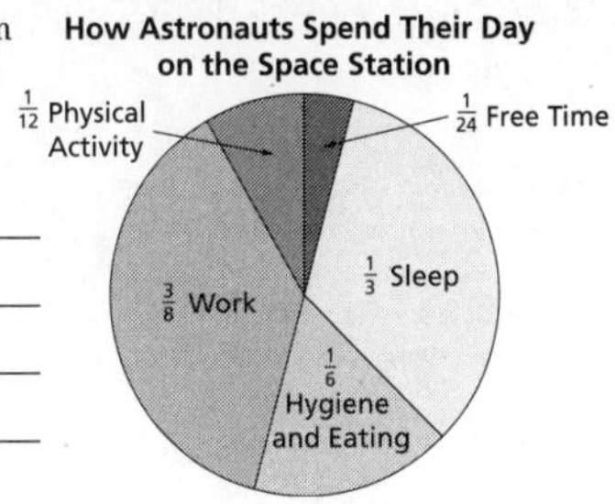

How Astronauts Spend Their Day on the Space Station

$\frac{1}{12}$ Physical Activity

$\frac{1}{24}$ Free Time

$\frac{1}{3}$ Sleep

$\frac{3}{8}$ Work

$\frac{1}{6}$ Hygiene and Eating

Plan • Multiply 24 by $\frac{3}{8}$.

_____

_____

_____

_____

Try Show your work. Write your answer as a complete sentence.

$$\frac{\overset{3}{\cancel{24}}}{1} \times \frac{3}{\cancel{8}_{1}} = \frac{9}{1}$$
$$= 9$$

An astronaut works 9 hours per day.

---

8. The space station is in orbit 210 miles above Earth. This is 137 miles less than the distance from San Francisco to Los Angeles. What is the distance between those two cities? ◂MAH 120

Did you know?
Most jets rarely go higher than 8 miles above the Earth. Military jets travel 20 miles above the Earth.

Plan • Add 210 to 137.

• The answer will be in miles.

_____

Try Show your work. Write your answer as a complete sentence.

```
   210
 + 137
   347
```

The distance between San Francisco and Los Angeles is 347 miles.

more ▸

65

Discussing the Exercises

When going over the exercises, allow time for class discussion.

6. *What information is* not *needed to solve the problem?* (The average American uses about 160 gallons of water per day.)

8. *How might you use a picture to help you solve this problem?*

Possible answer:

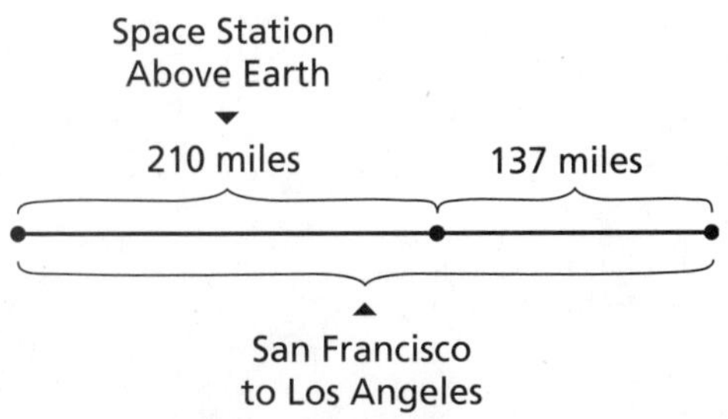

Space Station
Above Earth
▾

210 miles   137 miles

●———————————●———————————●

▲

San Francisco
to Los Angeles

Objectives

Read for understanding.

Plan and carry out a solution to a problem.

Understand that there may be more than one way to correctly solve a problem.

Using Math at Hand

References to handbook items appear with the following exercises.

Exercise 9 Items 086 and 008 (Multiplying with Multiples of 10; Comparing Whole Numbers)

Exercise 10 Items 131–133 (Subtracting with Regrouping)

Exercise 11 Item 135 (Subtracting with Decimals)

Exercise 12 Item 298 (Circumference)

There is often more than one good plan for solving a problem.

This table shows some facts about Earth and Mars.

Comparisons	Earth	Mars
Average Distance from the Sun	93,000,000 miles	142,000,000 miles
Solar Revolution in Earth Days	365.24 days	686.65 days
Diameter	7,926 miles	4,220 miles
Surface Temperature	⁻94°F to ⁺130°F	⁻185°F to ⁺77°F
Number of Moons	1	2

Use the information from the table to solve each problem. **Sample answers are provided.**

9. Is the average distance from Mars to the sun more than twice the average distance from Earth to the sun? ◄MAH 086, 008

Plan
- **Multiply 93,000,000 by 2.**
- **Compare the product to 142,000,000.**

Try Show your work. Write your answer as a complete sentence.

93,000,000 × 2 = 186,000,000

186,000,000 > 142,000,000

The average distance from Mars to the sun is not more than twice the average distance from Earth to the sun.

10. Because Mars is farther from the sun than Earth is, it is colder on Mars than on Earth. Find the difference between the maximum temperature on Earth and the maximum temperature on Mars. ◄MAH 131–133

Plan
- **Subtract 77 from 130.**
- **The answer will be in degrees Fahrenheit.**

Try Show your work. Write your answer as a complete sentence.

130 − 77 = 53

The difference between maximum temperatures is 53°F.

66   Vocabulary ▼ maximum

Exercises: Getting Started

Have students work independently or in small groups on the exercises on pages 66–67. Be sure they understand that they will need to use the information in the table for the problems on both pages.

11. Because Mars is farther from the sun than Earth is, it takes longer to revolve around the sun. How much longer does it take Mars to revolve around the sun than it takes Earth to revolve around the sun? ◂MAH 135

Plan • Subtract 365.24 from 686.65.

• The answer will be in days.

Try Show your work. Write your answer as a complete sentence.

$$
\begin{array}{r}
686.65 \\
- 365.24 \\
\hline
321.41
\end{array}
$$

It takes Mars 321.41 days longer than it takes Earth to revolve around the sun.

---

12. Find the length of Earth's equator. (Use 3.14 for π.) Is this more or less than the length of the Martian equator? ◂MAH 298

Plan • Use the formula for circumference: π*d*.

Earth: 3.14 × 7926

Mars: 3.14 × 4220

• Compare circumferences.

diameter

equator

Try Show your work. Write your answers as complete sentences.

$$
\begin{array}{r}
7926 \\
\times 3.14 \\
\hline
24{,}887.64
\end{array}
\qquad
\begin{array}{r}
4220 \\
\times 3.14 \\
\hline
13{,}250.80
\end{array}
\qquad 24{,}887.64 > 13{,}250.80
$$

Earth's equator is about 24,887.64 miles long. This is longer than Mars' equator.

more ▸

© Great Source. Copying is prohibited.

Vocabulary

diameter

maximum

pi (π)

Direct students to the vocabulary words at the bottom of each page. Have them find the words on the pages and circle them. Then have them go to the Vocabulary section of the student book, starting on page 108. Ask them to write and/or illustrate a definition for each word.

Encourage them to use *Math at Hand*, a dictionary, or a math textbook to help them write their definition.

If some students need help writing the correct definition, you may wish to share with them the sample definition given in this teacher's guide starting on page 108.

Discussing the Exercises

When going over the exercises, allow time for class discussion.

10. *What is meant by* the maximum temperature? (the highest the temperature has ever gotten)

12. *How is the length of the equator related to the diameter of Earth?* (The equator is a circle with a diameter equal to Earth's diameter. The circumference of the circle is the length of the equator. The circumference is approximately equal to 3.14 times the length of the diameter.) *How can you compare the two circumferences without calculating them both?* (Just compare the two diameters.)

© Great Source. Copying is prohibited.

Objectives

Read for understanding.

Plan and carry out a solution to a problem.

Understand that there may be more than one way to correctly solve a problem.

Using Math at Hand

References to handbook items appear with the following exercises.

Exercise 13 Item 170 (Multiplying Mixed Numbers)

Exercise 14 Item 086 (Multiplying with Multiples of 10)

Exercise 15 Items 142–143 (Multiplying with Decimals)

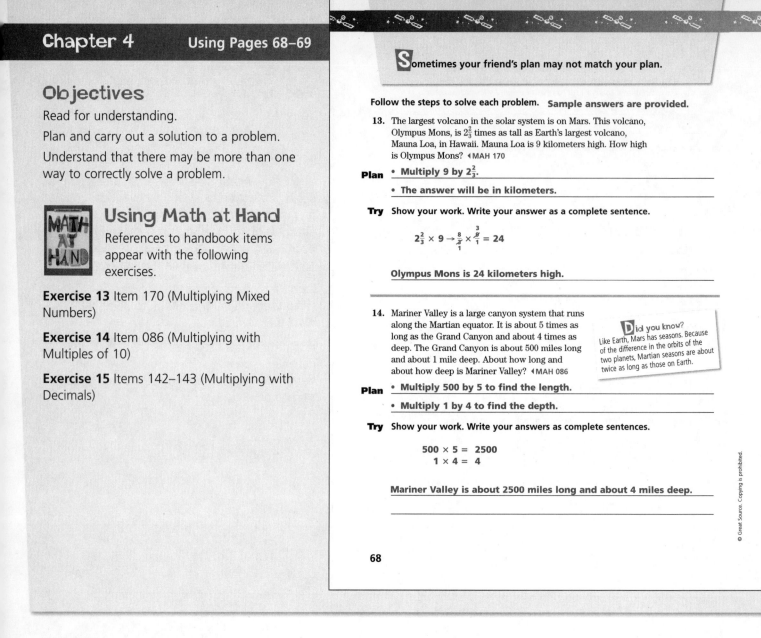

Sometimes your friend's plan may not match your plan.

Follow the steps to solve each problem.   Sample answers are provided.

13. The largest volcano in the solar system is on Mars. This volcano, Olympus Mons, is $2\frac{2}{3}$ times as tall as Earth's largest volcano, Mauna Loa, in Hawaii. Mauna Loa is 9 kilometers high. How high is Olympus Mons? ◄MAH 170

Plan • Multiply 9 by $2\frac{2}{3}$.

     • The answer will be in kilometers.

Try Show your work. Write your answer as a complete sentence.

$$2\frac{2}{3} \times 9 \rightarrow \frac{8}{3} \times \frac{\overset{3}{\cancel{9}}}{1} = 24$$

Olympus Mons is 24 kilometers high.

14. Mariner Valley is a large canyon system that runs along the Martian equator. It is about 5 times as long as the Grand Canyon and about 4 times as deep. The Grand Canyon is about 500 miles long and about 1 mile deep. About how long and about how deep is Mariner Valley? ◄MAH 086

Did you know?
Like Earth, Mars has seasons. Because of the difference in the orbits of the two planets, Martian seasons are about twice as long as those on Earth.

Plan • Multiply 500 by 5 to find the length.

     • Multiply 1 by 4 to find the depth.

Try Show your work. Write your answers as complete sentences.

$$500 \times 5 = 2500$$
$$1 \times 4 = 4$$

Mariner Valley is about 2500 miles long and about 4 miles deep.

68

Exercises: Getting Started

Have students work independently or in small groups on the exercises on pages 68–69.

15. Because Mars is smaller than Earth, the pull of gravity is less on Mars than on Earth. Your weight on Mars would be 0.375 times your weight on Earth. If Maria's weight on Earth is 96 pounds, what is her weight on Mars? ◂MAH 142–143

Plan • **Multiply 96 by 0.375.**

Try Show your work. Write your answer as a complete sentence.

$$\begin{array}{r} 0.375 \\ \times\ 96 \\ \hline 2250 \\ +\ 33750 \\ \hline 36.000 \end{array}$$

Maria's weight on Mars is 36 pounds.

It's now time for you to decide. Go back and read page 54 again. If this were a real contest, would you like to win the trip to Mars? On the lines below, tell in 25 words or less why you *would* or *would not* like to make the trip.

Check students' work.

Answers to SPACE QUIZ on page 56:
1.C 2.B 3.D 4.C 5.D

69

Optional Follow Up

Make a bulletin board display. Title the display *Would You Like to Take a Trip to Mars*? Have each student copy his or her response to the question on page 69 onto a piece of paper, then illustrate it. Hang the responses on the bulletin board under the question.

Discussing the Exercises

When going over the exercises, allow time for class discussion.

13. *Which is taller, Olympus Mons or Mauna Loa?* (Olympus Mons)

15. *Is Maria's weight on Mars more or less than her weight on Earth?* (less)

Have students share their responses to the question *Would you like to win a trip to Mars?*

Assessment

Two forms of the chapter test are available: the test on these two student pages and the test provided on the copymasters on pages 128–129 of this teacher's guide.

You can use these two forms of the test in the way that works best for you.

- Use one test as a pretest and the other as a posttest.
- Use one test as a practice test and one for assessment.
- Use one test as assessment and the other for a make-up test for students who were absent or who did poorly and need a chance to try again.

Fill in the circle with the letter of the correct answer.

1. Riki answers 3 out of 10 questions incorrectly. Which equation would you use to find the fraction of the questions Riki answered correctly?

   (A) $\frac{5}{5} - \frac{3}{5} = \frac{2}{5}$ (C) $\frac{3}{3} - \frac{1}{3} = \frac{2}{3}$

   (B) $\frac{10}{10} - \frac{3}{10} = \frac{7}{10}$ (D) $\frac{3}{10} - \frac{1}{10} = \frac{2}{10}$

For exercises 2–5, fill in the circle with the letter of the correct answer. Write your plan in the box.   Sample plans are provided.

2. Danya was present on 3 out of the 5 school days this week. What percent of the days was she present?

   (A) 30%   (C) 60%

   (B) 40%   (D) 35%

   - Write $\frac{3}{5}$ as a fraction with a denominator of 100.
   - The numerator of the new fraction shows the percent.

3. Mia's birthday is on April 27. Natalie's birthday is 9 days later. When is Natalie's birthday?

   (A) May 6   (C) April 36

   (B) May 7   (D) May 9

   - Find the number of days in April.
   - Subtract the number of April days from 9.
   - The difference is a date in May.

4. Mario weighs 84 pounds. His backpack weighs 5 pounds. How much does Mario weigh with his backpack on?

   (A) 89 pounds   (C) 81 pounds

   (B) 79 pounds   (D) 845 pounds

   - Add 84 and 5.
   - The answer is in pounds.

5. A class has 30 students. Four fifths of them go on a field trip. How many students do *not* go on the field trip?

   (A) 30 students   (C) 6 students

   (B) 45 students   (D) 24 students

   - Multiply 30 by $\frac{4}{5}$.
   - Subtract the product from 30.

70

Name _____ Date _____

Fill in the circle with the letter of the correct answer.

1. Lucy answers 7 out of 10 questions correctly. Which equation would you use to find the fraction of the questions Lucy answered incorrectly?

   (A) $\frac{10}{10} - \frac{7}{10} = \frac{3}{10}$ (C) $10 - 3 = 7$

   (B) $\frac{10}{10} - \frac{3}{10} = \frac{7}{10}$ (D) $10 - 7 = 3$

For exercises 2–5, fill in the circle with the letter of the correct answer. Write your plan in the box.

2. Terry was present on 4 out of the 5 school days this week. What percent of the days was she present?

   (A) 40%   (C) 80%

   (B) 20%   (D) 60%

3. Shawn's birthday is on April 29. Henri's birthday is 5 days later. When is Henri's birthday?

   (A) May 4   (C) April 34

   (B) May 5   (D) May 6

4. Heidi weighs 78 pounds. Her cat weighs 8 pounds. If Heidi stands on the scale holding her cat, what weight will be shown on the scale?

   (A) 70 pounds   (C) 78 pounds

   (B) 86 pounds   (D) 788 pounds

5. A choral group has 50 students. Two fifths of them are boys. How many students in the choral group are boys?

   (A) 30 students   (C) 50 students

   (B) 45 students   (D) 20 students

128

Name _____ Date _____

Fill in the circle with the letter of the correct answer. Explain why you made your choice.

6. A truck weighs 5,000 pounds. Which word expression describes how to write 5000 pounds as tons?

   (A) 5,000 pounds ÷ 2,000 pounds per ton _____

   (B) 5,000 pounds × 2,000 pounds per ton _____

7. A box is 40 inches long and 15 inches wide. It is $\frac{1}{2}$ as deep as it is long. Which word expression describes how to find the volume of the box?

   (A) 40 inches × 15 inches × 20 inches _____

   (B) 40 inches × 15 inches × 40 inches _____

   (C) 40 inches × 15 inches × 30 inches _____

   (D) 40 inches × 15 inches × 7 1\2 inches _____

For exercises 8–9, write your answer on the lines.

8. Mr. Chang bought a used car that cost $12,400. The dealer deducted $2500 from the price because Mr. Chang traded in his old car. How much did Mr. Chang pay? Show your work.

   _____

   _____

9. Ellen plans to go away to soccer camp. The camp will last 27 days. She wants to know how many weeks that is. Ellen's work is at the right.

   What did Ellen do wrong? Show how you would find the exact number of weeks.

   Ellen
   27
   × 7
   189

   _____

   _____

   _____

70

Fill in the circle with the letter of the correct answer. Explain why you made your choice. Sample explanations are provided.

6. A truck weighs 2.5 tons. Which word expression describes how to write 2.5 tons as pounds?

Ⓐ 2.5 tons ÷ 2000 pounds per ton

Ⓑ 2.5 tons × 2000 pounds per ton

The number of pounds must be _more_ than the number of tons.

7. A swimming pool is 20 feet long and 15 feet wide. It is $\frac{1}{2}$ as deep as it is long. Which word expression describes how to find the volume of the pool?

Ⓐ 10 ft × 20 ft × 15 ft

Ⓑ 10 ft × 20 ft × 15 ft

Ⓒ 40 ft × 20 ft × 15 ft

Ⓓ 40 ft × 20 ft × 15 ft

The depth must be $\frac{1}{2}$ of 20, or 10 feet.

To find volume, multiply length times width times height.

For exercises 8–9, write your answer on the lines. Sample answers are provided.

8. Mr. Sands bought a used car that cost $10,500. The dealer deducted $2,500 from the price because Mr. Sands traded in his old car. How much did Mr. Sands pay? Show your work.

$$\begin{array}{r} 10,500 \\ -\ 2,500 \\ \hline 8,000 \end{array}$$

Mr. Sands paid $8,000.

9. Daniel plans to go away to a computer camp. The camp will last 23 days. He wants to know how many weeks that is. Daniel's work is at the right. What did Daniel do wrong? Show how you would find he exact number of weeks.

Daniel multiplied when he should have divided. He will be at camp for $3\frac{2}{7}$ weeks.

Daniel
$$\begin{array}{r} 23 \\ \times\ 7 \\ \hline 161 \end{array}$$

$$\begin{array}{r} 3\frac{2}{7} \\ 7\overline{)23} \\ -\ 21 \\ \hline 2 \end{array}$$

71

Ideas for Struggling Learners

- Pairs of students can find and evaluate more than one plan for each problem.
- Students can use highlighters to color-code words or phrases in text that relate to questions they need to answer.
- Students can point to and read aloud passages that may be challenging.
- Students can use the margins to jot down important information.
- Students can work in pairs to take turns. One reads a question and the other paraphrases it. When they're sure they understand the questions, they can work independently to complete the test.

Answers for Alternate Form Test

1. A

2. C
Possible Plan:
- Write $\frac{4}{5}$ as a fraction with a denominator of 100.
- The numerator of the new fraction shows the percent.

3. A
Possible Plan:
- 1 day later is April 30.
- The remaining 4 days are in May.

4. B
Possible Plan:
- Add 78 and 8.
- The answer is in pounds.

5. D
Possible Plan:
- Multiply 50 by $\frac{2}{5}$.

6. A
Possible explanation: The number of tons must be less than the number of pounds.

7. A
Possible explanation: The depth is $\frac{1}{2}$ of 40 inches, or 20 inches. To find volume, multiply length by width by height.

8. $12,400
$$\begin{array}{r} -2,500 \\ \hline \$\ 9,900 \end{array}$$

Mr. Chang paid $9,900.

9. Ellen multiplied when she should have divided. She will be at camp for $3\frac{6}{7}$ weeks.

$$\begin{array}{r} 3\frac{6}{7} \\ 7\overline{)27} \\ -21 \\ \hline 6 \end{array}$$

Chapter 5

WILD EARTH: VOLCANOES
Looking Back

WILD EARTH: VOLCANOES
Looking Back

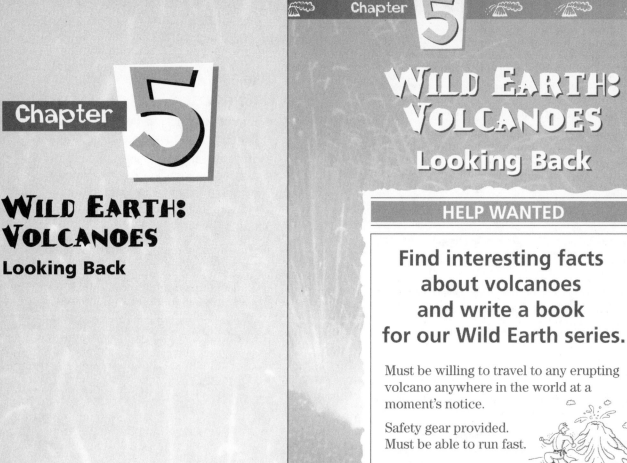

HELP WANTED

Find interesting facts about volcanoes and write a book for our Wild Earth series.

Must be willing to travel to any erupting volcano anywhere in the world at a moment's notice.

Safety gear provided.
Must be able to run fast.

Our Planet Publishing Company

72

Using Pages 72–73

Guiding the Reading

Students should read these two pages independently. Use the copymaster on page 120 of this book to help guide their reading. You may need to explain what is meant by *molten*. Molten refers to a solid that has been made liquid by very high heat.

Connecting to the Theme

These are optional ideas for connecting to the theme of volcanoes as you do this chapter.

• Have the students become volcanologists. Have them form small groups and prepare reports about different volcanoes.

• Have students research the legends and folklore about volcanoes.

• Have students study other possible wild-Earth topics, such as hurricanes, tornadoes, and earthquakes.

Bibliography

Clarkson, Peter. *Volcanoes.* Stillwater, MN: Voyageur Press, Inc., 2000.

Lauber, Patricia. *Volcano: The Eruption and Healing of Mount St. Helens.* New York: Bradbury Press, 1986.

Mattern, Joanne. *Mauna Loa: World's Largest Active Volcano.* New York: PowerKids Press, 2002.

In this chapter, you will be collecting information about volcanoes. You'll learn about volcanoes that have erupted recently, and you'll *look back* at volcanoes that erupted long ago. You'll also learn different ways to review your work on math problems, check your computation, and think about whether your answer is reasonable. You'll get plenty of practice using the fourth step of the four-step problem-solving method: **Look Back**.

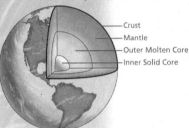

▼ The earth has an inner core, outer core, mantle, and crust. The mantle is hot and semi-molten. The temperature is about 2400°F. When there is too much pressure on the crust from the magma, or molten rock, the magma erupts to form a volcano.

— Crust
— Mantle
— Outer Molten Core
— Inner Solid Core

▲ The word *volcano* comes from Vulcan, the Roman god of fire.

▶ It is very difficult to predict the eruption of a volcano. Mount St. Helens was closely watched by scientists. They had noticed that it was more active in March of 1980. However, there was no warning before it erupted on May 18, 1980.

Vocabulary   semi-

73

Sample Answers for Reading Guide

1. Our Planet Publishing Company
2. Find interesting facts about volcanoes and write a book.
3. inner core, outer core, mantle, and crust
4. 2400°F
5. too much pressure on the core from the magma, or molten rock
6. from Vulcan, the Roman god of fire
7. No.
8. May 18
9. Look Back

Chapter 5   Reading Guide for Pages 72-73

Name _____ Date _____

1. What company is planning a book about volcanoes?
   _____

2. What is the company looking for someone to do?
   _____

3. What are the four layers that make up the earth?
   _____

4. What is the approximate temperature of the mantle? _____

5. What causes a volcano to erupt?
   _____

6. Where does the word *volcano* come from?
   _____

7. Is there always a warning before a volcano erupts? _____

8. What was the date of the 1980 eruption of Mount St. Helens?
   _____

9. Which problem-solving step will you practice in Chapter 5?
   _____

120

Websites

Volcano Expedition
http://www.sio.ucsd.edu/volcano/
   Go on a virtual volcano expedition in Costa Rica.

National Geographic: Eye in the Sky—Volcanoes
http://www.nationalgeographic.com/eye/volcanoes/volcanoes.html
   This site includes information on many natural events, including volcanoes.

Volcano World
http://www.volcanoworld.org/
   Great photos and information about volcanoes

Vocabulary

semi-

Direct students to the vocabulary at the bottom of page 73. Have them find the prefix on the page and circle it. Then have them go to the Vocabulary section of the student book, starting on page 108. Ask them to write and/or illustrate a definition for the prefix.

Encourage them to use *Math at Hand*, a dictionary, or a math textbook to help them write their definition.

Objective

Read critically to be sure that questions asked are questions answered.

Using Math at Hand

References to handbook items appear with the following exercises.

Exercise 1 Items 133 and 008 (Regrouping Across Zeros; Comparing Whole Numbers)

Exercise 2 Items 322 and 327 (Time; Changing from One Unit to Another)

Exercise 3 Items 033 and 037 (Fraction of a Set; Simplest Form)

Exercise 4 Item 005 (Reading and Writing Large Numbers)

Exercise 5 Items 020 and 015 (Relating Decimals to Percents; Equivalent Decimals)

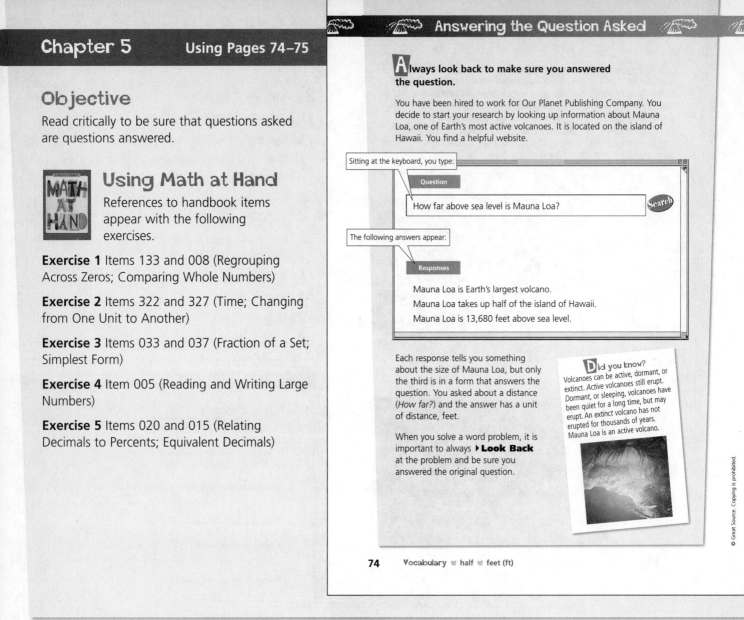

Answering the Question Asked

Always look back to make sure you answered the question.

You have been hired to work for Our Planet Publishing Company. You decide to start your research by looking up information about Mauna Loa, one of Earth's most active volcanoes. It is located on the island of Hawaii. You find a helpful website.

Sitting at the keyboard, you type:

Question

How far above sea level is Mauna Loa?

Search

The following answers appear:

Responses

Mauna Loa is Earth's largest volcano.
Mauna Loa takes up half of the island of Hawaii.
Mauna Loa is 13,680 feet above sea level.

Each response tells you something about the size of Mauna Loa, but only the third is in a form that answers the question. You asked about a distance (*How far?*) and the answer has a unit of distance, feet.

When you solve a word problem, it is important to always ▶ **Look Back** at the problem and be sure you answered the original question.

Did you know?

Volcanoes can be active, dormant, or extinct. *Active* volcanoes still erupt. *Dormant*, or sleeping, volcanoes have been quiet for a long time, but may erupt. An *extinct* volcano has not erupted for thousands of years. Mauna Loa is an active volcano.

74   Vocabulary ◾ half ◾ feet (ft)

Beginning the Lesson

Read the introduction yourself or have a student volunteer read it aloud.

Use the following questions to check students' understanding of the introduction.

- *Which sentence in the Responses gives the answer to the question asked?* (Mauna Loa is 13,680 feet above sea level.)

- *If a volcano is described as active, what does that mean?* (It still erupts.)

- *Are all volcanoes active?* (No.)

Exercises: Getting Started

Have students work independently or in small groups on the exercises on pages 74–75.

Circle the choice that answers the question asked.

1. The top of Mauna Loa is 13,680 feet above sea level. The rest of it is under the ocean! The total height is 56,000 feet. How much more of Mauna Loa is below sea level than above sea level? ◂MAH 133, 008

   A. Mauna Loa is already 42,320 feet high at sea level.

   B. Mauna Loa's under-sea measure is 28,640 feet greater than its above-sea measure.

2. Mauna Loa's longest eruption lasted for 18 months. How many years was that? ◂MAH 322, 327

   A. 1.5 years

   B. 78 weeks

3. There are about 550 active volcanoes in the world. Every year about 50 of them erupt. About what fraction of active volcanoes erupt each year? ◂MAH 033, 037

   A. About $\frac{1}{11}$ of the world's active volcanoes erupt each year.

   B. About $\frac{10}{11}$ of the world's active volcanoes do not erupt each year.

4. Edinburgh Castle in Scotland is built on the remains of a volcano that has been extinct for three hundred twenty-five million years. Which of the following shows three hundred twenty-five million written as a numeral? ◂MAH 005

   A. 3 hundred 25 million

   B. 325,000,000

5. When volcanoes erupt, sulfur dioxide is produced. This causes acid rain, which can kill trees and poison life in ponds, rivers, and lakes. About 20 percent of the sulfur dioxide in the air comes from volcanoes. Which decimal represents 20%? ◂MAH 020, 015

   A. 0.2

   B. $\frac{20}{100}$

more ▸

Vocabulary ▾ million ▾ numeral ▾ decimal

75

Vocabulary

decimal	million
feet (ft)	numeral
half	

Direct students to the vocabulary words at the bottom of each page. Have them find the words on the pages and circle them. Then have them go to the Vocabulary section of the student book, starting on page 108. Ask them to write and/or illustrate a definition for each word.

Encourage them to use *Math at Hand*, a dictionary, or a math textbook to help them write their definition.

If some students need help writing the correct definitions, you may wish to share with them the sample definitions given in this teacher's guide starting on page 108.

Discussing the Exercises

When going over the exercises, allow time for class discussion. Be sure students realize that, while both answer choices for the exercises are true, they are *not* both answers to the question.

1. Have a volunteer draw a picture to represent this problem.

2. *Why could you eliminate choice B?* (The answer must be in years, not weeks.)

Extending the Lesson: Solving the Problems

You may wish to have students show how they would solve the problems. Be sure to have them check that their solutions match the answers they circled on page 75.

Objectives

Scan for labels, words, or symbols that flag relevant information in problems.

Select correct answers from among true facts.

Using Math at Hand

References to handbook items appear with the following exercises.

Exercise 6 Item 010 (Ordering Whole Numbers)

Exercise 7 Items 010 and 132 (Ordering Whole Numbers; Subtracting with Regrouping)

Exercises 8–9 Item 122 (Adding with Regrouping)

Exercise 10 Item 010 (Ordering Whole Numbers)

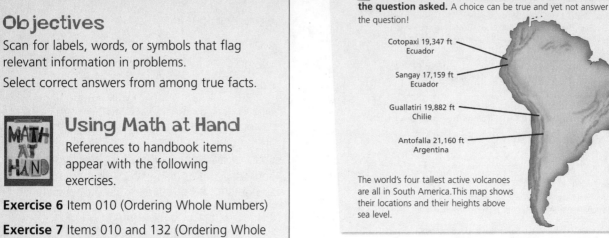

Think about why an answer choice would not match the question asked. A choice can be true and yet not answer the question!

Cotopaxi 19,347 ft
Ecuador

Sangay 17,159 ft
Ecuador

Guallatiri 19,882 ft
Chilie

Antofalla 21,160 ft
Argentina

The world's four tallest active volcanoes are all in South America. This map shows their locations and their heights above sea level.

Use the map. For exercises 6–10, circle the choice that answers the question asked.

6. What is the altitude of the tallest active volcano? ◄MAH 010

   A. Antofalla

   B. 21,160 feet

7. What is the difference in altitude between the two highest active volcanoes? ◄MAH 010, 133

   A. Antofalla and Guallatiri

   B. 1,278 feet

8. Which volcano is 2,723 feet taller than Sangay? ◄MAH 122

   A. Guallatiri is 2,723 feet taller than Sangay.

   B. Guallatiri is 535 feet taller than Cotopaxi.

76

Exercises: Getting Started

Have students work independently or in small groups on the exercises on pages 76–77. Be sure students understand that while the answer choices are all true, only one in each pair answers the question asked.

9. Mount Everest is the tallest mountain in the world. It is 7875 feet taller than Antofalla. What is the altitude of Mount Everest? ◀MAH 122

   A. Mount Everest is 29,035 feet tall.

   B. Mount Everest is more than 8000 feet taller than Guallatiri.

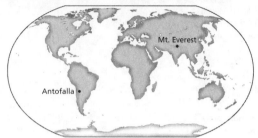

10. List the altitudes of the 4 tallest active volcanoes in order from greatest to least. ◀MAH 010

   A. Antofalla, Guallatiri, Cotopaxi, Sangay

   B. 21,160 ft; 19,882 ft; 19,347 ft; 17,159 ft

11. Look back at exercises 6 and 9. Tell why you made the answer choices you did. **Sample answers are provided.**

Exercise 6   **The answer must be a measurement, not a name.**

Exercise 9   **The answer must be the height of Mt. Everest, not a comparison.**

You now see that it's important to check your answer. Always compare your answer to the original problem to be sure you've answered the question.

Vocabulary ▾ least ▾ greatest   77

Vocabulary

least

greatest

Direct students to the vocabulary words at the bottom of page 77. Have them find each word on the page and circle it. Then have them go to the Vocabulary section of the student book, starting on page 108. Ask them to write and/or illustrate a definition for the words.

Encourage them to use *Math at Hand*, a dictionary, or a math textbook to help them write their definition.

If some students need help writing correct definitions, you may wish to share with them the sample definitions given in this teacher's guide starting on page 108.

Optional Follow Up

Have students make a bar graph that shows the heights of the four highest active volcanoes.

Discussing the Exercises

When going over the exercises, allow time for class discussion.

7. *How did you decide which choice was the answer?* (The problem asked for the difference in altitude, so I knew the answer had to be a measurement.)

8. *How did you decide which choice was the answer?* (The problem asks for a volcano taller than Sangay, not taller than Cotopaxi.)

10. *How did you decide which choice was the answer?* (I knew I needed a list of altitudes, not a list of volcanoes.)

Extending the Lesson: Solving the Problems

You may wish to have students write plans and show the worked-out solutions for problems 7–9. Be sure to have them check that their solutions match the answers they circled.

Objective

Critically read questions and answer choices to eliminate unreasonable answer choices.

Materials

Calculators (for optional solving of problem 7)

Using Math at Hand

References to handbook items appear with the following exercise.

Exercises 1–2 Items 168 and 147 (Multiplying a Whole Number by a Fraction; Division without Remainders)

Exercise 4 Item 132 (Subtracting with Regrouping)

Exercise 5 Item 130 (Subtracting without Regrouping)

Exercise 6 Items 135 and 016 (Subtracting with Decimals; Comparing Decimals)

Exercise 7 Item 447 (Using a Calculator to Compute with Whole Numbers)

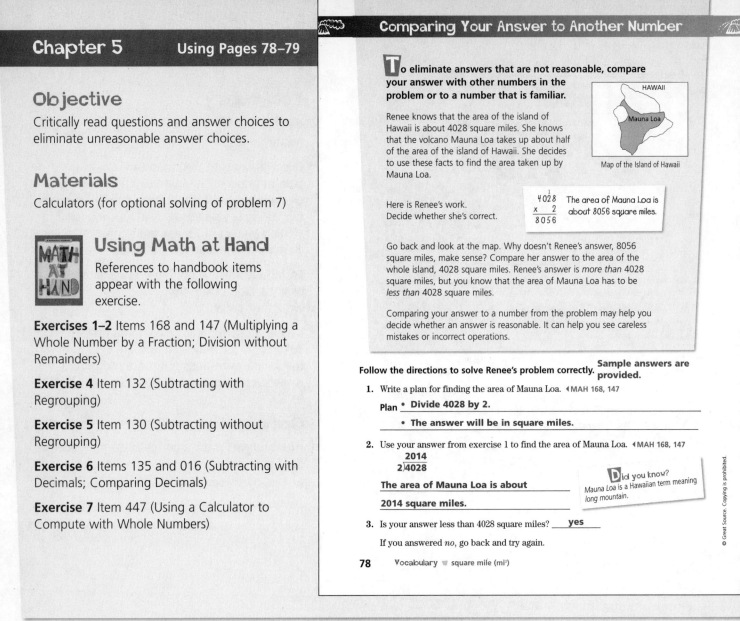

Comparing Your Answer to Another Number

To eliminate answers that are not reasonable, compare your answer with other numbers in the problem or to a number that is familiar.

Renee knows that the area of the island of Hawaii is about 4028 square miles. She knows that the volcano Mauna Loa takes up about half of the area of the island of Hawaii. She decides to use these facts to find the area taken up by Mauna Loa.

Here is Renee's work. Decide whether she's correct.

$$\begin{array}{r} \overset{1}{4028} \\ \times\ \ 2 \\ \hline 8056 \end{array}$$

The area of Mauna Loa is about 8056 square miles.

Go back and look at the map. Why doesn't Renee's answer, 8056 square miles, make sense? Compare her answer to the area of the whole island, 4028 square miles. Renee's answer is *more than* 4028 square miles, but you know that the area of Mauna Loa has to be *less than* 4028 square miles.

Comparing your answer to a number from the problem may help you decide whether an answer is reasonable. It can help you see careless mistakes or incorrect operations.

Follow the directions to solve Renee's problem correctly. **Sample answers are provided.**

1. Write a plan for finding the area of Mauna Loa. ◄MAH 168, 147

   Plan • **Divide 4028 by 2.**

       • **The answer will be in square miles.**

2. Use your answer from exercise 1 to find the area of Mauna Loa. ◄MAH 168, 147

   $$2\overline{)4028} \quad 2014$$

   The area of Mauna Loa is about 2014 square miles.

   Did you know? Mauna Loa is a Hawaiian term meaning long mountain.

3. Is your answer less than 4028 square miles? ___**yes**___

   If you answered *no*, go back and try again.

78   Vocabulary ▾ square mile (mi²)

Beginning the Lesson

Read the introduction yourself or have a student volunteer read it aloud.

Use the following question to check students' understanding of the introduction.

- *How do you know that the area of Mauna Loa must be less than 4028 square miles?* (The shaded area on the map represents Mauna Loa. It takes up only part of the island which has an area of 4028 square miles.)

Exercises 1–3 on page 78 can be done as a class activity. Some students may choose to multiply 4028 by $\frac{1}{2}$. Other students may choose to divide 4028 by 2. You may wish to have students demonstrate that the two are equivalent.

Exercises: Getting Started

Have students work independently or in small groups on the exercises on page 79.

Be sure students understand that it is not necessary for them to solve the problem. They just need to use their answer to the **THINK** question to help them cross out two answers which could not possibly be correct.

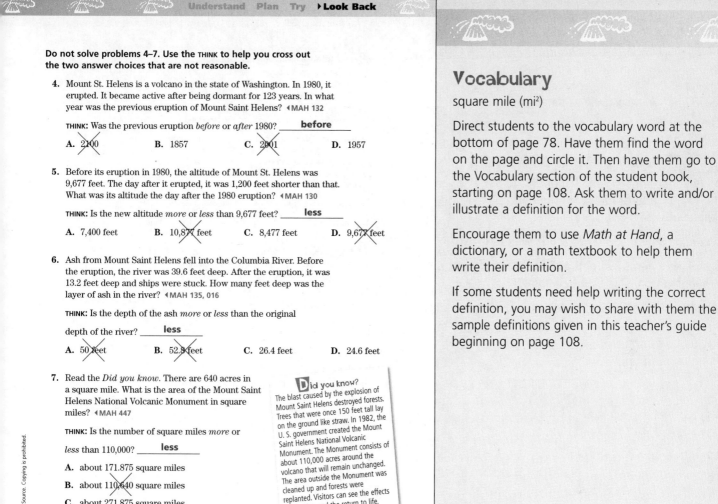

Do not solve problems 4–7. Use the THINK to help you cross out the two answer choices that are not reasonable.

4. Mount St. Helens is a volcano in the state of Washington. In 1980, it erupted. It became active after being dormant for 123 years. In what year was the previous eruption of Mount Saint Helens? ◂MAH 132

   THINK: Was the previous eruption *before* or *after* 1980? ___**before**___

   A. 2100   B. 1857   C. 2001   D. 1957

5. Before its eruption in 1980, the altitude of Mount St. Helens was 9,677 feet. The day after it erupted, it was 1,200 feet shorter than that. What was its altitude the day after the 1980 eruption? ◂MAH 130

   THINK: Is the new altitude *more* or *less* than 9,677 feet? ___**less**___

   A. 7,400 feet   B. 10,877 feet   C. 8,477 feet   D. 9,677 feet

6. Ash from Mount Saint Helens fell into the Columbia River. Before the eruption, the river was 39.6 feet deep. After the eruption, it was 13.2 feet deep and ships were stuck. How many feet deep was the layer of ash in the river? ◂MAH 135, 016

   THINK: Is the depth of the ash *more* or *less* than the original depth of the river? ___**less**___

   A. 50 feet   B. 52.8 feet   C. 26.4 feet   D. 24.6 feet

7. Read the *Did you know.* There are 640 acres in a square mile. What is the area of the Mount Saint Helens National Volcanic Monument in square miles? ◂MAH 447

   THINK: Is the number of square miles *more* or *less* than 110,000? ___**less**___

   A. about 171.875 square miles
   B. about 110,640 square miles
   C. about 271.875 square miles
   D. about 610,000 square miles

   Did you know?
   The blast caused by the explosion of Mount Saint Helens destroyed forests. Trees that were once 150 feet tall lay on the ground like straw. In 1982, the U. S. government created the Mount Saint Helens National Volcanic Monument. The Monument consists of about 110,000 acres around the volcano that will remain unchanged. The area outside the Monument was cleaned up and forests were replanted. Visitors can see the effects of eruption and the return to life.

   more ▸

79

Vocabulary

square mile (mi²)

Direct students to the vocabulary word at the bottom of page 78. Have them find the word on the page and circle it. Then have them go to the Vocabulary section of the student book, starting on page 108. Ask them to write and/or illustrate a definition for the word.

Encourage them to use *Math at Hand*, a dictionary, or a math textbook to help them write their definition.

If some students need help writing the correct definition, you may wish to share with them the sample definitions given in this teacher's guide beginning on page 108.

Discussing the Exercises

When going over the exercises, allow time for class discussion.

4. If students have difficulty with this problem, you may need to explain that *the previous eruption* would be an eruption that occurred just before the volcano became dormant for 123 years.

5. You may wish to have students draw a picture to represent this problem.

6. You may wish to have students draw a picture to represent this problem.

When crossing out answers, some students may think that 50 is less than 39.6. This means that they do not understand place value of decimal numbers. Point out that 50 is equivalent to 50.0.

7. If you choose to have students solve this problem, allow them to use calculators, if available.

Extending the Lesson: Solving the Problems

You may wish to have students use a separate piece of paper to solve the problems.

4. B   6. C
5. C   7. A

Objective

Read and reread actively to determine reasonableness of answers.

Using Math at Hand

References to handbook items appear with the following exercises.

Exercise 8 Item 135 (Subtracting with Decimals)

Exercise 9 Items 294 and 327 (Length; Changing from One Unit to Another)

Exercise 10 Item 322 (Time)

Ask a question to help you decide whether an answer is reasonable.

Do not solve problems 8–10. Use the THINK to help you cross out the two answer choices that are not reasonable.

8. Until August of 1883, the island of Krakatoa in Indonesia was 5.4 miles long. It had 3 volcanoes. On August 27, there were 5 explosions. Hot ash and rock swept across the island and out to sea. After it was all over, the island was 3.6 miles shorter. What was the length of the island then? ◄MAH 135

   THINK: Is the answer *more* or *less* than 5.4 miles? _____**less**_____

   A. 9 miles   B. 8.1 miles   C. 2.2 miles   D. 1.8 miles

9. A volcanic eruption can cause *tsunamis*, a group of huge waves that move across the ocean. The eruptions on the island of Krakatoa caused tsunamis up to 132 feet high. What is that height in yards? ◄MAH 294, 327

   THINK: Is the number of yards *more* or *less* than 132? _____**less**_____

   A. 44 yards   B. 135 yards   C. 369 yards   D. 43 yards

10. A tsunami can travel 480 miles per hour. How many miles can it travel in a minute? ◄MAH 322

    THINK: Does the wave travel more miles in an hour or in a minute? _____ **in an hour** _____

    A. 28,800 miles

    B. 80 miles

    C. 2880 miles

    D. 8 miles

Did you know?
The word *tsunami* comes from Japan. It was made from two Japanese words: *tsu* which means harbor, and *nami* which means wave.

80

Exercises: Getting Started

Have students work independently or in small groups on the exercises on pages 80–81.

Be sure students understand that it is not necessary for them to solve the problem. They just need to use their answer to the THINK question to help them cross out two answers which could not possibly be correct.

Write the word *tsunami* on the board. Model the correct pronunciation: soo NAH mee.

Look back at problems 8–10 to answer each question.   **Sample answers are provided.**

11. How did you decide whether your answer to problem 8 was *more* or *less* than 5.4 miles?

The island became shorter, so the length had to be less

than before.

12. How did you decide whether your answer to problem 9 was *more* or *less* than 132 yards?

A yard is longer than a foot, so fewer yards than feet

measure the same distance.

13. Look back at problem 10. How did you decide whether the wave travels more miles in an hour or in a minute?

A minute is shorter than an hour, so the distance traveled in a

minute must be less than the distance traveled in an hour.

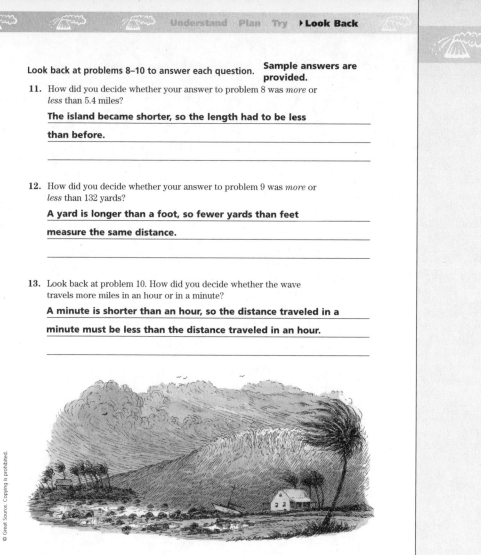

81

Discussing the Exercises

When going over the exercises, allow time for class discussion.

8. You may wish to have students draw a picture to represent this problem.

9. *What fact do you need to know to solve this problem?* (1 yard = 3 feet) *Is a yard longer or shorter than a foot?* (longer) *Is the same distance measured by more yards or more feet?* (more feet)

10. *What fact do you need to know to solve this problem?* (1 hour = 60 minutes) *Is a minute longer or shorter than an hour?* (shorter) *Is the same rate measured by more miles per minute or more miles per hour?* (more miles per hour)

11. A picture may make it easier for students to explain why the answer is less than 5.4 miles.

12–13. Look carefully at students' answers. Students will often forget whether to multiply or divide when solving problems like these. Understanding what the magnitude of their answer should be will help them choose the correct operation.

Extending the Lesson: Solving the Problems

You may wish to have students use a separate piece of paper to solve the problems.

   8. D

   9. A

   10. D

Objective
Read critically to be sure that answers are correctly labeled.

Using Math at Hand
References to handbook items appear with the following exercises.

Exercise 1 Items 367 (Circles); 299 (Area); 305 (Area of Circles); 169 (Multiplying a Fraction by a Fraction)

Exercise 2 Items 319–320 (Temperature); 139 (Multiplying Whole Numbers)

Exercise 3 Item 132 (Subtracting without Regrouping)

Exercise 4 Items 294 (Length); 327 (Changing from One Unit to Another); 149 (Interpreting Quotients and Remainders)

Always look back to be sure your answer is complete.

You log on to the United States Geologic Survey website (www.usgs.gov). There, you find interesting volcano facts, including the volume of 5 volcanoes from the island of Hawaii. Before logging off, you write the information on a note card.

Volcanoes on the Island of Hawaii	
Volcano	Approximate Volume
Mauna Loa	80,000
Mauna Kea	30,000
Kilauea	30,000
Hualalai	12,400
Kohala	14,000

Later, you realize that you have forgotten to put units with the numbers. Because volume is a measure, it needs units to be meaningful.

You know that the numbers must show *cubic* units since they represent *volume*. But you can't remember whether they are cubic *miles* or cubic *kilometers*.

A *cubic mile* is the amount of space taken up by a cube 1 mile long, 1 mile wide, and 1 mile high.

A *cubic kilometer* is the amount of space taken up by a cube 1 kilometer long, 1 kilometer wide, and 1 kilometer high.

There is a big difference between cubic miles and cubic kilometers! A cubic mile is equivalent to about 4 cubic kilometers. You should realize how important it is to label measures with the correct units.

You go back to the website and find out that the numbers represent cubic kilometers.

82 Vocabulary ▾ cubic mile (mi³) ▾ cubic kilometer (km³)

Exercises: Getting Started

Have students work independently or in small groups on the exercises on page 83. Be sure they understand that, for exercises 1 and 2, they should choose the correct label from the box and that, for exercises 3 and 4, they should write a label for each answer.

Choose the correct unit from the box to answer exercises 1–2.

1. The diameter of the circular crater at the top of Mauna Loa is $2\frac{1}{4}$ miles. What is the area of the crater? Round the answer to the nearest whole number. ◀MAH 367, 299, 305, 169

diameter

| miles |
| square miles |
| cubic miles |

Answer 4 _____ square miles

2. Water boils at 212°F. Lava from a volcano can be 15 times that hot. How hot can lava from a volcano be? ◀MAH 319–320, 139

| °F |
| °C |
| degrees |

Answer 3180 _____ °F

Write a correct unit in the answer for exercises 3–4.

3. In the year 79 A.D., Mount Vesuvius erupted violently, burying the city of Pompeii. It was not until 1707 A.D. that the city was rediscovered. A farmer digging a well struck the top of a wall from the city. About how long was it between the eruption and the farmer's discovery? ◀MAH 132

Answer about 1628 _____ years

4. In Pompeii, heavy rains hardened the ash into solid concrete. The city was buried in a layer of concrete 23 feet deep. Write this amount using different units. ◀MAH 294, 327, 149

Answer $7\frac{2}{3}$ _____ yards

These ruins are part of a city called Pompeii which was once covered in volcanic ash.

Did you know?
The lost city of Pompeii has been very interesting to scientists. Body-shaped holes showed where people had been struck down. Everyday objects such as bread, fruit, tables, and jewelry were found near them. The findings gave us a valuable look at life in ancient times.

more ▶

Vocabulary ▼ circular

83

Vocabulary

circular

cubic kilometer (km³)

cubic mile (mi³)

Direct students to the vocabulary words at the bottom of each page. Have them find the words on the pages and circle them. Then have them go to the Vocabulary section of the student book, starting on page 108. Ask them to write and/or illustrate a definition for each word.

Encourage them to use *Math at Hand*, a dictionary, or a math textbook to help them write their definition.

If some students need help writing the correct definitions, you may wish to share with them the sample definitions given in this teacher's guide starting on page 108.

Discussing the Exercises

When going over the exercises, allow time for class discussion.

2. *What does °F mean?* (degrees Fahrenheit)

4. Students should use estimation to help them determine the correct label. You may wish to help students find the answer in inches as well (276 in.)

Extending the Lesson: Solving the Problems

You may wish to have students write plans and show the worked-out solutions on a separate piece of paper. Be sure to have them check that their solutions match the answers given on page 83.

Objectives

Read critically.

Use estimation to check answers to problems.

Using Math at Hand

References to handbook items appear with the following exercises.

Exercise 1 Items 044 and 193 (Relating Fractions to Percents; Finding a Percent of a Number)

Exercise 2 Item 170 (Multiplying Mixed Numbers)

Exercise 3 Items 301 and 106–107 (Area of Squares and other Rectangles; Estimating Products)

Using Estimation to Check Your Answer

An estimate can help you decide whether your answer is about the right size.

While you are doing all your research on volcanoes, the people at Our Planet Publishing Company are busy working on other details for the book.

Using estimation can help you decide whether your answer to a problem makes sense. An estimate can't tell you for sure if your answer is correct, but it can help you spot big errors.

Follow the steps to rule out answer choices that are not reasonable.

1. Mount Fuji is a dormant volcano. Katsushika Hokusai was a Japanese painter and wood engraver. A print from one of his woodcarvings of Mount Fuji will be used on the cover of the book. Our Planet Publishing Company chooses two of the prints and conducts a survey of 500 people to see which print people prefer.

   The results show that 79% of the people prefer *Fine Wind, Clear Morning*. How many of the 500 people chose that print? ◄MAH 044, 193

Rainstorm Beneath the Summit

Fine Wind, Clear Morning

Circle the expression that gives the best estimate of the number of people who chose *Fine Wind, Clear Morning*.

A. $\left(\frac{4}{5} \times 500\right)$ **B.** 8×500 **C.** $\frac{1}{5} \times 500$ **D.** $\frac{1}{2} \times 500$

What is your estimate for the answer? About _____400_____ people

Use your estimate to cross out two answer choices that are not reasonable.

A. 395 people   **B.** 385 people   **C.** ~~250 people~~   **D.** ~~105 people~~

84   Vocabulary ▼ survey

Exercises: Getting Started

Have students work independently or in small groups on the exercises on pages 84–85.

Write *Katsushika Hokusai* on the board. Model the pronunciation: kat-s'-SHEE-kah HOH-k'-sahy.

Be sure students understand that it is not necessary to solve the problems. They just need to cross out two answers which could not possibly be correct.

2. The print of *Fine Wind, Clear Morning* that will appear on the cover will be $8\frac{1}{2}$ inches wide. If the height of the print is $\frac{3}{4}$ of its width, what will be the height of the print? ◄MAH 170

Circle the expression that gives the best estimate of the height in inches.

A. $\left(\frac{3}{4} \times 8\right)$ B. $\frac{3}{4} \times 80$ C. $\frac{3}{4} \times 6$ D. $\frac{3}{4} \times 800$

What is your estimate for the height? About _____**6 inches**_____

Use your estimate to cross out two answer choices that are not reasonable.

A. $6\frac{1}{2}$ inches   B. $60\frac{5}{8}$ inches   C. $6\frac{3}{8}$ inches   D. $60\frac{1}{8}$ inches

---

3. The dimensions of the original print of *Fine Wind, Clear Morning* are 36 centimeters by 27 centimeters. What is the area of the original print? ◄MAH 301, 106–107

Circle the expression that gives the best estimate of the area in square centimeters.

A. $\left(40 \times 30\right)$ C. $40 + 40 + 30 + 30$

B. $40 + 30$ D. 30×20

What is your estimate for the area? About _____**1200 square centimeters**_____

Use your estimate to cross out two answer choices that are not reasonable.

A. 912 cm²   B. 134 cm²   C. 72 cm²   D. 972 cm²

Katsushika Hokusai (1760–1849)

more ▶

Vocabulary

length of a rectangle

survey

width of a rectangle

Direct students to the vocabulary words at the bottom of each page. Have them find the words on the pages and circle them. Then have them go to the Vocabulary section of the student book, starting on page 108. Ask them to write and/or illustrate a definition for the word.

Encourage them to use *Math at Hand*, a dictionary, or a math textbook to help them write their definition.

If some students need help writing the correct definition, you may wish to share with them the sample definition given in this teacher's guide beginning on page 108.

Discussing the Exercises

When going over the exercises, allow time for class discussion.

3. Students may be surprised to see how far off a useful estimate can be.

Extending the Lesson: Solving the Problems

You may wish to have students use a separate piece of paper to solve the problems.

1. A
2. C
3. D

Objectives

Read critically.

Use estimation to rule out unreasonable answer choices.

Using Math at Hand

References to handbook items appear with the following exercises.

Exercise 4 Items 101 and 129–132 (Rounding to Estimate Sums and Differences; Subtracting Whole Numbers)

Exercise 5 Items 260 and 112–113 (Mean or Average; Estimating Quotients Using Compatible Numbers)

Exercise 6 Items 101 and 130 (Rounding to Estimate Sums and Differences; Subtracting without Regrouping)

Exercise 7 Items 260 and 113 (Mean or Average; Estimating Quotients Using Compatible Numbers)

When you estimate, sometimes you use rounded numbers and sometimes you use compatible numbers.

Follow the steps to rule out answer choices that are not reasonable.

4. The book will have a total of 192 pages. The introduction will be 9 pages long. Then there will be 5 chapters and a glossary. The chapters and the glossary take up how many pages? ◂MAH 101, 129–132

   Circle the expression that gives the best estimate of the number of pages for the chapters and the glossary.

   A. (190 − 10)   **B.** 190 − 5   **C.** 190 + 10   **D.** 190 + 5

   What is your estimate for the answer? About ____**180 pages**____

   Use your estimate to cross out two answer choices that are not reasonable.

   A. 38 ~~pages~~   **B.** 201 ~~pages~~   **C.** 181 pages   **D.** 183 pages

---

5. The plan is to have 408 photos in the book. If the book has 192 pages, what will be the average number of photos per page? ◂MAH 260, 112–113

   Circle the expression that uses compatible numbers to estimate the average number of photos per page.

   A. (400 ÷ 200)   **B.** 410 ÷ 190   **C.** 408 ÷ 192   **D.** 400 ÷ 190

   What is your estimate for the average number of photos per page?

   About ____**2 photos**____

   Use your estimate to cross out two answer choices that are not reasonable.

   A. $20\frac{3}{8}$ ~~photos~~

   B. $2\frac{1}{8}$ photos

   C. $2\frac{3}{8}$ photos

   D. $21\frac{3}{8}$ ~~photos~~

Exercises: Getting Started

Have students work independently or in small groups on the exercises on pages 86–87.

Be sure students understand that it is not necessary for them to solve the problems. They just need to use their estimates to help them cross out two answers that could not possibly be correct.

Sample answers are provided.

6. Chapter 4 of the book will begin on page 118 and end on page 149. How many pages are in Chapter 4? ◂ MAH 101, 130

   Write an expression that gives a good estimate of the answer.

   _____ 150 − 120 _____

   What is your estimate for the answer? About _____ 30 pages _____

   Use your estimate to cross out two answer choices that are not reasonable.

   A. ~~3 pages~~   B. 32 pages   C. 31 pages   D. ~~52 pages~~

---

7. The editors have 156 words that they would like to include in the glossary. Eight pages are planned for the glossary. If they are able to include all 156 words, what will be the average number of glossary words per page? ◂ MAH 260, 113

   Use compatible numbers to estimate the answer.

   160 ÷ 8 = 20

   Explain how you chose the compatible numbers.

   160 is close to 156 and is divisible by 8. _____

   _____

   Use your estimate to cross out two answer choices that are not reasonable.

   A. 19.4 words   C. 195 ~~words~~

   B. 19.5 words   D. 194 ~~words~~

   You look forward to seeing the book when it comes out.

   Wild Earth
   Volcanoes

   Our Planet Publishing Company
   by _____
   (your name)

   87

Vocabulary

estimate (verb)

Direct students to the vocabulary word at the bottom of page 86. Have them the word on the page and circle it. Then have them go to the Vocabulary section of the student book, starting on page 108. Ask them to write and/or illustrate a definition for the word.

Encourage them to use *Math at Hand*, a dictionary, or a math textbook to help them write their definition.

If some students need help writing the correct definitions, you may wish to share with them the sample definitions given in this teacher's guide beginning on page 108.

Discussing the Exercises

When going over the exercises, allow time for class discussion.

5. Some students may be puzzled by the fact that the average number of photos per page is not a whole number. Explain that, even when all pieces of data are whole numbers, the average may not be. For example, they may sometimes see the average number of children per family in the U.S. expressed as a mixed decimal.

6. If your students try to solve this problem, be sure they see that, since *both first and last* pages are included in these numbers, 149 − 118 will *not* give them the correct answer. A simpler problem should help: first page 1 and last page 2 is 2 pages, not 1 page.

Extending the Lesson: Solving the Problems

You may wish to have students use a separate piece of paper to solve the problems.

4. D   6. B
5. B   7. B

Assessment

Two forms of the chapter test are available: the test on these two student pages and the test provided on the copymasters on pages 130–131 of this teacher's guide.

You can use these two forms of the test in the way that works best for you.

- Use one test as a pretest and the other as a posttest.
- Use one test as a practice test and one for assessment.
- Use one test as assessment and the other for a make-up test for students who were absent or who did poorly and need a chance to try again.

Fill in the circle with the letter of the correct answer.

1. You correctly find the volume of your classroom. Which of the following would label your answer?

   (A) square feet   (C) ● cubic feet

   (B) feet   (D) yards

2. The length of a rug is $1\frac{1}{3}$ times its width. The rug is 9 feet wide. Which of the following best describes the length of the rug?

   (A) 9 feet   (C) less than 9 feet

   (B) ● more than 9 feet   (D) none of these

3. Michaela drove home at an average speed of 30 miles per hour. Which of the following is true about her speed in miles per minute?

   (A) It is 30 miles per minute.

   (B) It is more than 30 miles per minute.

   (C) ● It is less than 30 miles per minute.

   (D) none of these

4. A room is 15 feet long and 20 feet wide. Which unit best labels the area of the room?

   (A) ● square feet   (C) cubic feet

   (B) feet   (D) none of these

5. You read 11 books in 5 days. How many books per day is that?
   (HINT: Use estimation to choose the most reasonable answer.)

   (A) ● 2.2 books per day   (C) 0.22 books per day

   (B) 22 books per day   (D) 220 books per day

Name _____ Date _____

Fill in the circle with the letter of the correct answer.

1. You correctly find the volume of a suitcase. Which of the following would label your answer?

   (A) square feet   (C) feet

   (B) cubic feet   (D) pounds

2. The length of a photo is $1\frac{1}{3}$ times its width. The photo is 3 inches wide. Which of the following best describes the length of the photo?

   (A) 3 inches   (C) more than 3 inches

   (B) less than 3 inches   (D) none of these

3. Naomi drove home at an average speed of 25 miles per hour. Which of the following is true about her speed in miles per minute?

   (A) It is 25 miles per minute.

   (B) It is more than 25 miles per minute.

   (C) It is less than 25 miles per minute.

   (D) none of these

4. A pizza has a diameter of 12 inches. Which unit best labels the area of the pizza?

   (A) inches   (C) cubic inches

   (B) square inches   (D) none of these

5. Emily makes handbags out of duct tape. If she makes 9 bags in 4 days, how many bags per day does she average? (HINT: Use estimation to choose the most reasonable answer.)

   (A) 2.25 bags per day   (C) 0.225 bags per day

   (B) 225 bags per day   (D) 22.5 bags per day

Fill in the circle with the letter of the correct answer. Tell why you made your choice.

6. A circular rug has a radius of 4 feet. What is the area of the rug?
   (HINT: Use estimation to choose the most reasonable answer.)

   (A) 5024 square fee _____

   (B) 502.4 square feet _____

   (C) 5.024 square feet _____

   (D) 50.24 square feet _____

For exercises 7–9, write the answer on the lines provided.

7. Alaska has an area of 663,267 square miles. Texas has an area of 268,581 square miles. Write an expression that describes an estimate of the difference between the two areas.

   _____

8. A rope is 247 inches long. About how many feet long is it? Show your work.

   _____

   _____

9. Describe two ways you can look back at the solution to a problem to check it.

   _____

   _____

   _____

   _____

Fill in the circle with the letter of the correct answer. Tell why you made your choice.

6. A circular table has a diameter of 6 feet. What is the area of the table top?

   (HINT: Use estimation to choose the most reasonable answer.)

   (A) 28.26 square feet

   (B) 282.6 square feet

   (C) 2.82 square feet

   (D) 0.2826 square feet

   Sample answer:

   $r = 3$ ft

   $A = \pi r^2$, so the area is about 3×9 or 27 ft².

For exercises 7–9, write the answer on the lines provided.   **Sample answers are provided.**

7. Lake Superior has an area of 31,699 square miles. Lake Michigan has an area of 22,278 square miles. Write an expression that describes an estimate of the difference between the two areas.

   30,000 – 20,000

8. Angel Waterfall in Venezuela is 3281 feet high. About how many yards high is it? Show your work.

   3000 ÷ 3 = 1000

   Angel Waterfall is about 1000 feet high.

9. Describe two ways you can look back at the solution to a problem to check it.

   1. I can check to be sure my answer matches the question.

   2. I can use estimation to check my calculation.

89

Ideas for Struggling Learners

- Students can use highlighters to color-code words or phrases in text that relate to questions they need to answer.
- Students can point to and read aloud passages that may be challenging.
- Students can use the margins to jot down important information.
- Students can work in pairs to take turns. One reads a question and the other paraphrases it. When they're sure they understand the questions, they can work independently to complete the test.

Answers for Alternate Form Test

1. B
2. C
3. C
4. B
5. A
6. D Sample explanation:

   $r = 4$ ft

   $A = \pi r^2$, so the area is about 3×16 or 48 ft².

7. Sample answer: $700,000 - 300,000$
8. Sample answer: $240 \div 12 = 20$

   The rope is about 20 feet long.

9. Sample answer:

   1. I can check to be sure that my answer matches the question.

   2. I can use estimation to check my calculation.

Chapter 6

LAZY R HORSE RANCH

Putting It All Together

LAZY R HORSE RANCH
Putting It All Together

Come to
Lazy R Horse Ranch

Learn to:
- measure a horse
- feed a horse
- groom a horse
- ride a horse

90

Using Pages 90–91

Guiding the Reading

Students should read these two pages independently. Use the copymaster on page 121 of this book to help guide their reading.

Connecting to the Theme

These are optional ideas for connecting to the theme of horses as you do this chapter.

- Have the students work in small groups. Have each group take a time or event in history when horses were important to the economy. Have them prepare a report or presentation.

- Have students write an essay about what life would be like now if we used horses instead of cars and trucks.

Bibliography

Edwards, Elwyn Hartley. *The Ultimate Horse Book*. New York: Dorling Kindersley, Inc., 1991.

Prichard, Louise. *My Pony Book*. New York: DK Publishing, Inc., 1998.

Ransford, Sandy. *Horse and Pony Care*. New York: Kingfisher, 2002.

Horses have been very important in history and are still important in our lives. In this chapter, you will see that taking care of a horse is not simple. An organized method is needed. You'll learn how an organized method can also help you solve math problems. You'll put together all the skills you've learned so far to see how the four-step problem-solving method (**Understand, Plan, Try,** and **Look Back**) can help you become a better problem solver.

▶ In the 5th century B.C., the people in Persia rode horses to deliver messages. In the 19th century A.D., the United States used this method with the Pony Express.

Coming and Going of the Pony Express by Frederick Remington

▶ Workhorses had a major impact on history because they made it possible to take large amounts of produce and materials from village to village. In many parts of the world, and even in America, horses are still used to pull carts, wagons, and plows.

▲ When engines were invented to use in cars, trucks, and trains, people talked about their power in terms of the number of horses it took to exert the same force. We still use the word *horsepower* as a unit for measuring the power of engines.

91

Websites

Equine Web Page
http://www.ume.maine.edu/EQUINE/
Information on horses and their care.

Nature: Horses
http://www.pbs.org/wnet/nature/horses/
Information on horses and the way they have worked for people over the years.

Sample Answers for Reading Guide

1. Lazy R Horse Ranch
2. measure a horse, feed a horse, groom a horse, ride a horse
3. 19th century A.D.
4. Frederick Remington
5. They took large amounts of produce and materials from village to village
6. It refers to the number of horses it took to exert the same force as an engine.
7. Understand, Plan, Try, Look Back
8. Check students' work.

Chapter 6   Reading Guide for Pages 90–91

Name _____ Date _____

1. What is the name of the ranch you will be visiting?
   _____

2. What four things can you learn to do at Lazy R Horse Ranch?
   _____

3. In which century was the Pony Express used to deliver messages?
   _____

4. Who painted *Coming and Going of the Pony Express*?
   _____

5. What important role did workhorses play in history?
   _____
   _____

6. Where does the term *horsepower* come from?
   _____

7. In this chapter you will practice all four problem-solving steps. What are the four steps?
   _____

8. Have you ever helped take care of a horse? Do you think it would be a lot of work? Explain.
   _____
   _____
   _____
   _____
   _____

121

Objective

Summarize a passage.

Now it's time to apply what you've learned.

You arrive at Lazy R Horse Ranch. The wrangler's daughter, Kim, tells you that caring for a horse involves a lot more than feeding it a few apples and putting on a saddle. Here are just a few of the things she says.

- Cleanliness is very important for keeping horses healthy. Soiled straw bedding must be replaced daily. Fresh, clean water must be available at all times.

- Horses must be groomed daily. This keeps the hair clean, removes any insects that might feed on dead hair, and helps the horse's circulation. Each horse has its own grooming kit. This helps keep illnesses from spreading from horse to horse.

- Horses like to eat often. The amount of food each horse gets needs to be carefully calculated. The amount depends on the horse's weight and the amount of exercise it gets. The food must be carefully weighed.

- Each horse must get some exercise daily.

Kim also says that horses expect feeding, grooming, and exercise to follow a carefully-planned daily schedule.

Providing daily care helps Kim develop a special bond with her horses.

92

Beginning the Lesson

Read the introduction yourself or have a student volunteer read it aloud. Students may not be familiar with the word *wrangler*. A wrangler is another name for a cowboy, a person who herds horses and livestock on the range, but wrangler can also be used for a person who takes care of horses.

Use the following questions to check students' understanding of the introduction.

- *What kinds of things are important in caring for a horse?* (Possible answers: Keeping the horse and bedding clean; grooming the horse daily; feeding the horse the right amount of food; helping the horse exercise)

- *How is caring for a horse like problem solving?* (An organized method is needed.)

- *What are the steps in the four-step problem-solving method?* (Understand, Plan, Try, Look Back)

Exercises: Getting Started

Have students work independently or in small groups on the exercises on pages 93. Students may find it helpful to look back at the chapter introductions for chapters 1–5.

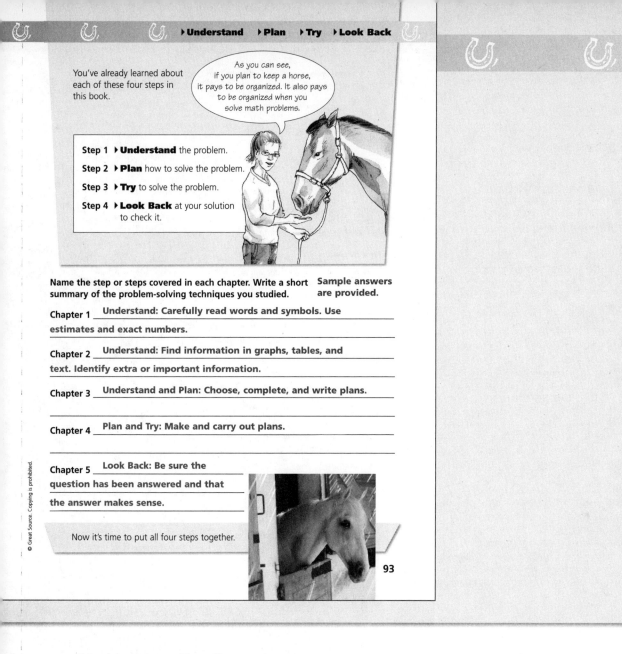

You've already learned about each of these four steps in this book.

As you can see, if you plan to keep a horse, it pays to be organized. It also pays to be organized when you solve math problems.

Step 1 ▶ **Understand** the problem.

Step 2 ▶ **Plan** how to solve the problem.

Step 3 ▶ **Try** to solve the problem.

Step 4 ▶ **Look Back** at your solution to check it.

Name the step or steps covered in each chapter. Write a short summary of the problem-solving techniques you studied.

Sample answers are provided.

Chapter 1 ___Understand: Carefully read words and symbols. Use estimates and exact numbers.___

Chapter 2 ___Understand: Find information in graphs, tables, and text. Identify extra or important information.___

Chapter 3 ___Understand and Plan: Choose, complete, and write plans.___

Chapter 4 ___Plan and Try: Make and carry out plans.___

Chapter 5 ___Look Back: Be sure the question has been answered and that the answer makes sense.___

Now it's time to put all four steps together.

93

Discussing the Exercises

When going over the exercises, allow time for class discussion. You may wish to make a composite list of student responses on the chalkboard.

Objectives

Read critically to sift out needed information.

Visualize the math in a problem.

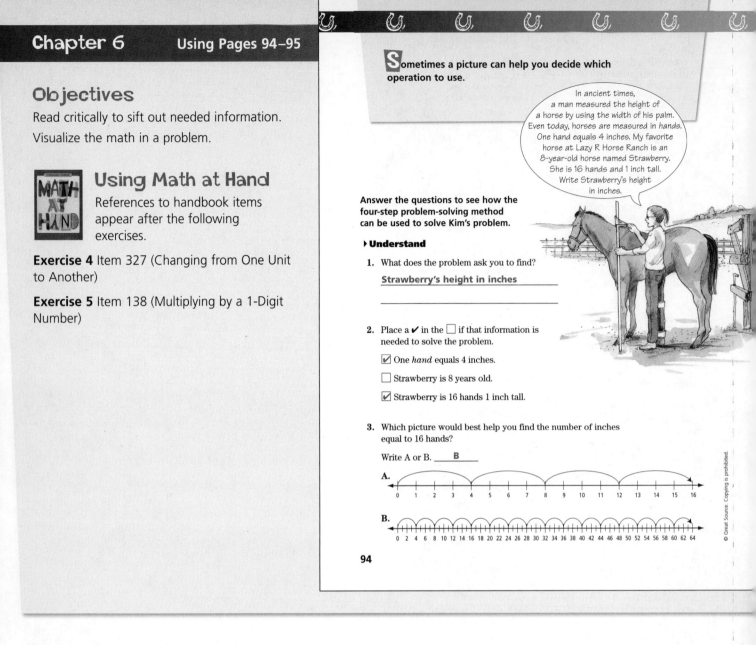

Using Math at Hand

References to handbook items appear after the following exercises.

Exercise 4 Item 327 (Changing from One Unit to Another)

Exercise 5 Item 138 (Multiplying by a 1-Digit Number)

Sometimes a picture can help you decide which operation to use.

In ancient times, a man measured the height of a horse by using the width of his palm. Even today, horses are measured in hands. One hand equals 4 inches. My favorite horse at Lazy R Horse Ranch is an 8-year-old horse named Strawberry. She is 16 hands and 1 inch tall. Write Strawberry's height in inches.

Answer the questions to see how the four-step problem-solving method can be used to solve Kim's problem.

▸ **Understand**

1. What does the problem ask you to find?

   Strawberry's height in inches
   _____

2. Place a ✔ in the ☐ if that information is needed to solve the problem.

   ☑ One *hand* equals 4 inches.

   ☐ Strawberry is 8 years old.

   ☑ Strawberry is 16 hands 1 inch tall.

3. Which picture would best help you find the number of inches equal to 16 hands?

   Write A or B. _____**B**_____

   A.
   0 1 2 3 4 5 6 7 8 9 10 11 12 13 14 15 16

   B.
   0 2 4 6 8 10 12 14 16 18 20 22 24 26 28 30 32 34 36 38 40 42 44 46 48 50 52 54 56 58 60 62 64

94

Exercises: Getting Started

Point out to students that exercises 1–9 refer to the problem Kim is asking at the top of page 94.

Have students work independently or in small groups on the exercises on pages 94–95.

4. Circle the plan that you could use to solve Kim's problem. ◂ MAH 327

> **Plan A**
> - Multiply 16 by 4.
> - Add 1 to the product.
> - The answer will be in inches.

Plan B
- Multiply 16 by 4.
- Subtract 1 from the product.
- The answer will be in inches.

▸ **Try**

5. Show the computation that you would use to carry out the plan. ◂ MAH 138

$$\begin{array}{r} 16 \\ \times\ 4 \\ \hline 64 \end{array} \qquad \begin{array}{r} 64 \\ +\ 1 \\ \hline 65 \end{array}$$

6. Write a sentence that tells the solution to Kim's problem.

Strawberry is 65 inches tall.

▸ **Look Back**   **For exercises 7–9, accept *No* if students went back and fixed their work.**

7. Did you answer the question that was asked? _____**Yes**_____

If you answered *no*, go back and redo your work.

8. Do you think your answer should be *more* or *less* than 16 inches? _____**More**_____

Is it? _____**Yes**_____

If you answered *no*, go back and check your work.

9. Does your answer have the correct units? _____**Yes**_____

If you answered *no*, go back and add or change the units.

more ▸

95

Optional Follow Up

Ask questions such as the following.

- *What is Strawberry's height in feet and inches?* (5 feet 5 inches)
- *What is 15 hands 3 inches in inches?* (63 inches)
- *What is your height in hands?* (Answers will vary.)

Discussing the Exercises

When going over the exercises, allow time for class discussion.

3. *Using the numbers 4 and 16, what expression could you use to describe picture A?* (16 ÷ 4) *Using the numbers 4 and 16, what expression could you use to describe picture B?* (16 × 4)

Objective

Translate from words to a math expression.

Materials

Calculators (if available)

Using Math at Hand

References to handbook items appear after the following exercises.

Exercise 12 Items 212–214 (Order of Operations)

Exercise 13 Items 137–141 and 146–151 (Multiplying with Whole Numbers; Dividing with Whole Numbers)

Exercise 17 Items 107 and 112 (Estimation)

Exercise 18 Items 086 and 092 (Multiplying with Multiples of 10; Dividing with Multiples of 10)

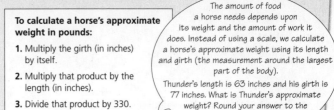

An estimate can sometimes help you decide whether you have made a careless mistake.

To calculate a horse's approximate weight in pounds:

1. Multiply the girth (in inches) by itself.
2. Multiply that product by the length (in inches).
3. Divide that product by 330.

The answer will be in pounds.

The amount of food a horse needs depends upon its weight and the amount of work it does. Instead of using a scale, we calculate a horse's approximate weight using its length and girth (the measurement around the largest part of the body). Thunder's length is 63 inches and his girth is 77 inches. What is Thunder's approximate weight? Round your answer to the nearest pound.

Answer the questions to see how the four-step problem-solving method can be used to solve Kim's problem.

▸ **Understand**

10. What does Kim's problem ask you to find?

    Thunder's approximate weight to the nearest pound

11. What information do you need to solve it?

    Thunder's length: 63 inches   Thunder's girth: 77 inches

▸ **Plan**

12. Circle the expression that you would use to find Thunder's approximate weight. ◂MAH 212–214

    A. $(77 \times 77 \times 63) \div 330$ **C.** $330 \div (77 \times 77 \times 63)$

    B. $(63 \times 63 \times 77) \div 330$ **D.** $330 \div (63 \times 63 \times 77)$

96

Exercises: Getting Started

Point out to students that exercises 10–19 refer to the problem at the top of page 96.

Have students work independently or in small groups on the exercises on pages 96–97.

▶ **Try**

13. Find the value of the expression you circled in exercise 12. Use a calculator if you have one. If you don't have a calculator, you can divide by 330 by first dividing by 33 and then dividing that quotient by 10. ◀ MAH 137–141, 146–151

   77 × 77 = 5929
   5929 × 63 = 373,527
   373,527 ÷ 330 = 1131.9

14. Write a sentence that tells the solution to the problem.

   Thunder weighs about 1132 pounds.

▶ **Look Back**   **For exercises 15–16, and 19, accept *No* if students went back and fixed their work.**

15. Did you answer the question that was asked? _____**Yes**_____

   If you answered *no*, go back and redo your work.

16. Does your answer have the correct units? _____**Yes**_____

   If you answered *no*, go back and add or change the units.

17. Circle the expression whose value is the best estimate for Thunder's weight in pounds. ◀ MAH 107, 112

   A. $(80 \times 80 \times 60) \div 30$ **C.** $300 \div (80 \times 80 \times 60)$

   B. $((80 \times 80 \times 60) \div 3) \div 100$ **D.** $300 \div (60 \times 60 \times 80)$

18. Use the expression you circled to estimate Thunder's weight. ◀ MAH 086, 092

   _____**1280 pounds**_____

19. Does your estimate show that your answer is reasonable? _____**Yes**_____

   If you answered *no*, go back and check your work.

   more ▶

Discussing the Exercises

When going over the exercises, allow time for class discussion.

13 and 17. *Why can you divide in two steps and get the same answer as dividing in one step?*
(Example: 330 = 33 × 10,
so 373,527 ÷ 330 = 373,527 ÷ (33 × 10).
If you divide by 33, then your quotient will be too great by a factor of 10.)

Objectives

Use information you know or you can look up to solve a problem.

Find and evaluate multiple ways to solve problems.

Using Math at Hand

References to handbook items appear after the following exercises.

Exercise 22 Item 322 (Time)

Exercise 24 Items 142–143 and 168 (Multiplying Decimals; Multiplying a Whole Number by a Fraction)

Sometimes, if information is missing from a problem, you may know the information or you may be able to look it up.

> Every day (including Saturday and Sunday) I groom Strawberry between 10:15 A.M. and 11:00 A.M. How many hours per week do I spend grooming Strawberry?

Answer the questions to see how the four-step problem-solving method can be used to solve Kim's problem.

▸ **Understand** Sample answers are provided.

20. What does the problem ask you to find?

Find the number of hours Kim spends

grooming Strawberry each week.

21. Place a ✔ in the ☐ if that information is needed to solve the problem.

☑ the number of days in a week

☐ the number of hours in a day

☑ the number of minutes in an hour

22. For each box you checked in exercise 21, write the information and tell how you found it. ◂MAH 322

I know that there are 7 days in a week.

I know that there are 60 minutes in an hour.

▸ **Plan**

23. Write a plan for solving Kim's problem.

Plan

• **Find the number of hours between 10:15 and 11.**

• **Multiply by 7.**

or

• **Find the number of minutes between 10:15 and 11.**

• **Multiply by 7.**

• **Divide the product by 60.**

98

Exercises: Getting Started

Point out to students that exercises 20–27 refer to the problem Kim is asking at the top of page 98.

Have students work independently or in small groups on the exercises on pages 98–99.

▸**Try**

24. Show how you would carry out the plan. ◂MAH 142–143, 168

10:15 to 11 is $\frac{3}{4}$ hour

$\frac{3}{4} \times 7 = \frac{21}{4} = 5\frac{1}{4}$

or

10:15 to 11 is 45 minutes

$45 \times 7 = 315$

$315 \div 60 = 5\frac{1}{4}$

25. Write a sentence that tells the solution to Kim's problem.

Kim grooms Strawberry $5\frac{1}{4}$ hours per week.

▸**Look Back**   **For exercises 26–27, accept *No* if students went back and fixed their work.**

26. Did you answer the question that was asked? _____ **Yes** _____

If you answered *no*, go back and redo your work.

27. Does your answer have the correct label? _____ **Yes** _____

If you answered *no*, go back and add or change the label.

Did you know?

There is a special way to carry out each step of horse grooming. To brush the horse's tail, stand to one side. Hold the tail in one hand and gradually let the hairs down until you have brushed the whole tail. Use your fingers and a body brush to untangle knots.

more ▸

99

Discussing the Exercises

When going over the exercises, allow time for class discussion.

23. Some students may choose to find the number of hours between 10:15 and 11:00 and then multiply by 7. Other students may find the number of minutes, multiply that by 7, and then divide by 60. Discuss these different ways of solving the problem.

24. If students choose to first find the time between 10:15 and 11:00 in hours, they may choose to write that time as either $\frac{3}{4}$ hour or 0.75 hour. Emphasize that either way will work. Have volunteers show that $\frac{3}{4} \times 7 = 5\frac{1}{4}$ and $0.75 \times 7 = 5.25$. Be sure students understand that the answers are equivalent.

Objective
Think about the magnitude of an answer in order to choose the correct operation.

Using Math at Hand
References to handbook items appear after the following exercise.

Exercise 31 Items 135 and 153–154 (Subtracting with Decimals; Dividing with Decimals)

When deciding whether to multiply or divide, think about how large or small the answer should be.

Answer the questions to see how the four-step problem-solving method can be used to solve Kim's problem. Sample answers are provided.

▶ **Understand**

> The best way to feed horses is to give them a little to eat several times during the day. Starlight gets 7.2 kilograms of food each day. Of this, 1.8 kilograms is hay and the rest is grain. I give her the grain in 4 equal feedings. What is the weight of each feeding of grain?

28. What does the problem ask you to find?

   <u>Find the weight of grain in</u>

   <u>each equal feeding.</u>

29. Is there any number in the problem that you don't need to solve the problem? <u>**No**</u>

   If *yes*, tell which number and why.

   _____

   _____

▶ **Plan**

30. Circle the plan that could be used to solve the problem.

   Plan A
   - Find the amount of hay fed each day.
   - Divide by 4.

   Plan B
   - Find the amount of grain fed each day.
   - Multiply by 4.

   Plan C
   - Find the amount of hay fed each day.
   - Multiply by 4.

   Plan D
   - Find the amount of grain fed each day.
   - Divide by 4.

100   Vocabulary ▬ kilogram (kg)

Exercises: Getting Started

Point out to students that exercises 28–36 refer to the problem Kim is asking at the top of page 100.

Have students work independently or in small groups on the exercises on pages 99–100.

▸**Try**

31. Show how you would carry out the plan. ◂MAH 135, 153–154

    Find the daily grain:

    7.2 (food)
    − 1.8 (hay)
    5.4 (grain)

    Find the grain in each feeding:

    $$\begin{array}{r} 1.35 \\ 4)\overline{5.40} \\ -400 \\ \hline 140 \\ -120 \\ \hline 20 \\ -20 \\ \hline 0 \end{array}$$

32. Write a sentence that tells the solution to the problem.

    The weight of each grain feeding is 1.35 kg.

▸**Look Back**   For exercises 33–34, and 36, accept *No* if students went back and fixed their work.

33. Did you answer the question that was asked? _____ **Yes** _____

    If you answered *no*, go back and redo your work.

34. Do you think your answer should be *more* or *less* than 7.2 kilograms?

    _____ **Less** _____

    Is it? _____ **Yes** _____ If you answered *no*, go back and check your work. ◂MAH 016

35. Explain how you decided whether your answer should be *more* or *less* than 7.2 kilograms.

    Since 7.2 kilograms is enough food for the whole day and since

    there is more than one feeding per day, each feeding must be

    ***less* than 7.2 kilograms.**

36. Does your answer have the correct units?

    _____ **Yes** _____

    If you answered *no*, go back and add or change the units.

    Did you know?
    When measuring a horse's food, use weight, not volume. A bushel of corn weighs more than a bushel of oats! You also need to be sure you don't count the weight of the container.

101

© Great Source. Copying is prohibited.

Vocabulary

kilogram (kg)

Direct students to the vocabulary word at the bottom of page 100. Have them find the word on the page and circle it. Then have them go to the Vocabulary section of the student book, starting on page 108. Ask them to write and/or illustrate a definition for the word.

Encourage them to use *Math at Hand*, a dictionary, or a math textbook to help them write their definition.

If some students need help writing the correct definition, you may wish to share with them the sample definitions given in this teacher's guide starting on page 108.

Discussing the Exercises

When going over the exercises, allow time for class discussion.

© Great Source. Copying is prohibited.

Objectives

Paraphrase to understand problems.

Plan and carry out solutions to problems.

Using Math at Hand

References to handbook items appear after the following exercise.

Exercise 1 Item 184 (Using Proportions to Solve Problems)

When solving problems on your own, you can always use the four-step method.

It won't solve the problem for you, but it can help you keep organized. Here are some questions to think about as you use this method.

▸ Understand

- Do I know what each word in the problem means? (If you don't know what a word means, use *Math at Hand*, the Vocabulary section of this book, your math book, or a dictionary to help you.)
- What information do I have?
- What do I need to find out?
- Should my answer be an estimate or an exact number?
- Can I draw a diagram to help me understand the problem?
- Is there any information that is missing? If so, can I find it?
- Is there extra information that I should ignore?

▸ Plan

- Can I draw a diagram to help me solve the problem?
- Can I write an expression or equation that shows what the problem says?
- Can I solve a simpler problem that will help me solve the original problem?
- Do I need to compute more than once?

▸ Try

- Am I carrying out each step of my plan?
- Am I using the correct information from the problem?
- Am I computing correctly?
- Is my plan working, or do I need to change it?

▸ Look Back

- Did I answer the question that was asked?
- Did I label my answer correctly?
- Can I check whether my answer makes sense by comparing it to one of the other numbers in the problem?
- Can I use estimation to check whether my answer is reasonable?

102

Beginning the Lesson

Read page 102 yourself or have a student volunteer read it aloud. Page 102 provides a list of questions students can ask themselves as they try to solve any problem. You may wish to make a poster with these questions so that students can refer to them any time they are solving problems. These questions sum up the many problem-solving skills and strategies students have studied while using this book.

Exercises: Getting Started

Explain to students that they should use the space provided to share their thoughts on how they solved the problem. They are not expected to answer every question posed on page 102. They should, however, write something under each of the four problem-solving steps.

Have students work independently or in small groups on the problem on page 103.

Solve the problem. Explain how you used each of the four problem-solving steps. Use the questions on page 102 to help you.   Solution strategies will vary.
Samples are provided.

1. The ratio of hay to energy-feed in a horse's diet depends on the amount of work the horse does. The horse doing light work will need more hay and less energy-feed, while the horse doing hard work will need less hay and more energy-feed. For average work, the ratio of hay to energy-feed is 5 to 3. An 1100-pound horse doing average work needs to eat 20 pounds of hay per day. How much energy-feed does it need per day? ◂ MAH 184

▸ **Understand**

I need to find the amount of energy-feed the horse needs

in one day.

▸ **Plan**

Write and solve a proportion: $\frac{hay}{energy\text{-}feed} = \frac{5}{3} = \frac{20}{?}$

▸ **Try**

$$\frac{5}{3} = \frac{20}{?}$$
$$5 \times ? = 3 \times 20$$
$$5 \times ? = 60$$
$$? = 60 \div 5$$
$$? = 12$$

Answer in a complete sentence.
The horse will need 12 pounds per day of energy-feed.

▸ **Look Back**

I know there must be more hay than energy-feed and there is:

20 > 12.

I labeled the answer correctly, in pounds.

more ▸

103

Optional Follow Up

You may wish to have students copy the questions on page 102 onto an index card using their best handwriting and adding some borders or decorations. They can then refer to the questions on this card any time they are solving problems. Or, ask for a volunteer to make a poster with these questions to display in the classroom.

Discussing the Exercises

When going over the problem, allow time for class discussion. You may wish to make a list of the different strategies students used to look back on their answers.

Objective
Explain solution strategies.

Using Math at Hand
References to handbook items appear after the following exercises.

Exercise 2 Items 301 (Area of Squares and Other Rectangles); 139 (Multiply Whole Numbers); 130 (Subtract without Regrouping),

Exercise 3 Items 367 (Circles); 298 (Circumference); 294 (Length)

Use everything you've learned so far to solve the problems.

Solve the problems. Explain how you used each of the four problem-solving steps. Use the questions on page 102 to help you.   Solution strategies will vary. Samples are provided.

2. On one side of the barn, there are large stalls that measure 16 feet by 16 feet. On the other side, there are small stalls that measure 12 feet by 10 feet. How much greater is the area of a large stall than the area of a small stall? ◄MAH 301, 139, 130

▶ **Understand**

I need to know the difference between two areas.

I know the length and width of each stall size.

▶ **Plan**

• Multiply to find the area of a large stall: 16×16.

• Multiply to find the area of a small stall: 12×10.

• Subtract to find the difference between the areas.

▶ **Try**

$$\begin{array}{r} 16 \\ \times\ 16 \\ \hline 96 \\ 160 \\ \hline 256 \end{array} \qquad 12 \times 10 = 120 \qquad \begin{array}{r} 256 \\ -\ 120 \\ \hline 136 \end{array}$$

Answer in a complete sentence.

The area of a large stall is 136 square feet greater than the area of a small stall.

▶ **Look Back**

I checked by re-doing my calculations.

I know my label is correct because feet $\times$ feet = square feet.

I answered the original question.

Exercises: Getting Started

Explain to students that they should use the space provided to share their thoughts on how they solved each problem. They are not expected to answer every question posed on page 102. They should, however, write something under each of the four problem-solving steps.

Have students work independently or in small groups on the problems on pages 104 and 105.

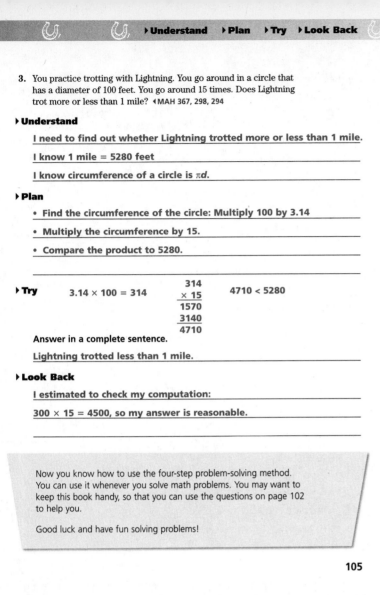

3. You practice trotting with Lightning. You go around in a circle that has a diameter of 100 feet. You go around 15 times. Does Lightning trot more or less than 1 mile? ◂MAH 367, 298, 294

▸**Understand**

I need to find out whether Lightning trotted more or less than 1 mile.

I know 1 mile = 5280 feet

I know circumference of a circle is πd.

▸**Plan**

• Find the circumference of the circle: Multiply 100 by 3.14

• Multiply the circumference by 15.

• Compare the product to 5280.

▸**Try** $3.14 \times 100 = 314$

$$\begin{array}{r} 314 \\ \times\ 15 \\ \hline 1570 \\ 3140 \\ \hline 4710 \end{array}$$

$4710 < 5280$

Answer in a complete sentence.

Lightning trotted less than 1 mile.

▸**Look Back**

I estimated to check my computation:

$300 \times 15 = 4500$, so my answer is reasonable.

Now you know how to use the four-step problem-solving method. You can use it whenever you solve math problems. You may want to keep this book handy, so that you can use the questions on page 102 to help you.

Good luck and have fun solving problems!

105

Discussing the Exercises

When going over the exercises, allow time for class discussion.

3. *What is diameter?* (the distance across a circle through the center) Have a student volunteer draw a circle with a diameter on the chalkboard. *What do you call the distance around a circle?* (the circumference) *How do you find the circumference?* (Multiply the length of the diameter by π.) *What is the value of π?* (about 3.14 or about $\frac{22}{7}$) *How many feet are in a mile?* (5280)

Assessment

Two forms of the chapter test are available: the test on these two student pages and the test provided on the copymasters on pages 132–133 of this teacher's guide.

You can use these two forms of the test in the way that works best for you.

- Use one test as a pretest and the other as a posttest.
- Use one test as a practice test and one for assessment.
- Use one test as assessment and the other as a make-up test for students who were absent or who did poorly and need a chance to try again.

Exercises 1–8 are about this problem.

About 2 miles from Natalie's house, there is a circular track that has a diameter of 200 feet. Natalie jogs around the track 10 times. How much more than 1 mile does Natalie jog?

For exercise 1–3, fill in the circle with the letter of the correct answer.

1. Which information from the problem is *not* needed to solve the problem?

    (A) The track is 2 miles from Natalie's house.

    (B) The circular track has a diameter of 200 feet.

    (C) Natalie jogs around the track 10 times.

2. Which additional information is *not* needed to solve the problem?

    (A) The value of π is approximately 3.14.

    (B) There are 3 feet in a yard.

    (C) There are 5280 feet in a mile.

3. Which of the following best shows *a circular track that has a diameter of 200 feet?*

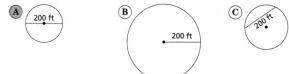

4. Fill in numbers to complete the plan that could be used to solve the original problem.

    Plan

    - Find the distance around the track in feet.

        Multiply ____200____ by ____3.14____.

    - Multiply the distance around the track by ____10____.

    - Subtract to compare the product to ____5280____.

Name _____ Date _____

Exercises 1–8 are about this problem.

Gen rides her bike to school 3 days each week. The front wheel on her bike has a diameter of 2 feet. When she rides from her house to school, her front wheel goes around 725 times. About how much less than a mile does Gen live from school?

For exercise 1–3, fill in the circle with the letter of the correct answer.

1. Which information from the problem is not needed to solve the problem?

    (A) Gen rides her bike to school 3 days each week.

    (B) The front wheel on her bike has a diameter of 2 feet.

    (C) When she rides from her house to school, her front wheel goes around 725 times.

2. Which additional information is *not* needed to solve the problem?

    (A) There are 5280 feet in a mile.

    (B) There are 3 feet in a yard.

    (C) The value of π is approximately 3.14.

3. Which of the following best shows *a bike wheel that has a diameter of 2 feet?*

    (A) 2 ft   (B) 2 ft   (C) 2 ft

4. Fill in numbers to complete the plan that could be used to solve the original problem.

    Plan

    - Find the circumference of the tire: Multiply _____ by _____.

    - Multiply the circumference of the tire by _____.

    - Subtract the product from _____.

Name _____ Date _____

5. Carry out the plan from exercise 4.

6. Write a sentence that gives the correct answer to the original problem. Be sure to include the units with the number.

    _____

7. Explain how you could use estimation to check that the distance from Gen's house to school that you calculated makes sense.

    _____
    _____

8. What are the four problem-solving steps? Choose one of the steps. Tell why you think that step is important.

    _____
    _____
    _____
    _____
    _____
    _____
    _____
    _____
    _____
    _____
    _____
    _____

5. Carry out the plan from exercise 4.

$3.14 \times 200 = 628$

$628 \times 10 = 6280$

$6280 - 5280 = 1000$

6. Write a sentence that gives the correct answer to the original problem. Be sure to include the units with the number.

Natalie jogs about 1000 feet more than 1 mile.

7. Explain how you could use estimation to check that your calculation of the distance around the track makes sense.

3.14×200 is about 3×200.

628 is close to 600.

8. What are the four problem-solving steps? Choose one of the steps. Tell why you think that step is important.

Check students' work.

107

Ideas for Struggling Learners

- Students can use scratch paper to work out a simpler problem

- Students can point to and read aloud passages that may be challenging.

- Pairs of students can try to find different plans that work and discuss which plan is easier to use.

- Students can work in pairs to take turns. One reads a question and the other paraphrases it. When they are sure that they understand the questions, they can work independently to complete the test.

Answers for Alternate Form Test

1. A
2. B
3. A
4. 2; 3.14; 725; 5280
5. $3.14 \times 2 = 6.28$.

   $725 \times 6.28 = 4553$

   $5280 - 4553 = 727$
6. Gen lives about 727 feet less than a mile from school.
7. 3.14×2 is about 3×2, or 6.

   725×6 is about 700×6, or 4200.

   4200 is close to 4553.
8. Check students' work.

Vocabulary

Sample entries are provided. Check students examples and diagrams.

A **approximately**

Near, but not exact.

area

The measure, in square units, of the space enclosed by a 2-dimensional figure or the surface of a 3-dimensional figure.

average

A single number that describes all the numbers in a set. The average is obtained by adding all the numbers and dividing that sum by the number of numbers.

B **base in exponential notation**

The number used as the factor in for example, 3^2. The base is 3 and the exponent is 2.

base of a pyramid

The face of the pyramid that contains one end of the altitude (segment from vertex, perpendicular to base). The only face of a pyramid that may not be a triangle.

base of a triangle

The side of a triangle that contains one end of an altitude (height); any side of a triangle can be called the base.

108

C **Celsius**

Temperature scale for the metric system of measurement. The freezing point of water at sea level is 0°C and the boiling point of water at sea level is 100°C.

century

100 years.

circle graph

A graph in which segments of a circle show how parts of a body of information are related.

circular

Having a round shape.

compatible number

A number that is easy to compute with using mental math.

109

cubic foot (ft³)

The volume of a cube with dimensions 1 ft × 1 ft × 1 ft.

cubic kilometer (km³)

The volume of a cube with dimensions 1 km × 1 km × 1 km.

cubic mile (mi³)

The volume of a cube with dimensions 1 mi × 1 mi × 1 mi.

D **decimal**

A number written using place value (tenths, hundredths, thousandths, etc.). A number containing a decimal point, or the decimal point itself.

degree (temperature)

Unit of measurement for temperature. Celsius and Fahrenheit are scales on which to read temperature.

denominator

The quantity below the line in a fraction. It tells the number of equal parts into which a whole is divided. In the fraction $\frac{5}{8}$, the denominator is 8.

110

diameter

A line segment that goes through the center of a circle and has endpoints on the circle.

difference

The amount that remains after one quantity is subtracted from another.

double bar graph

A graph with pairs of bars used to compare sets of data.

dozen

12 items.

E **estimate (*verb*)**

To find a number close to an exact number.

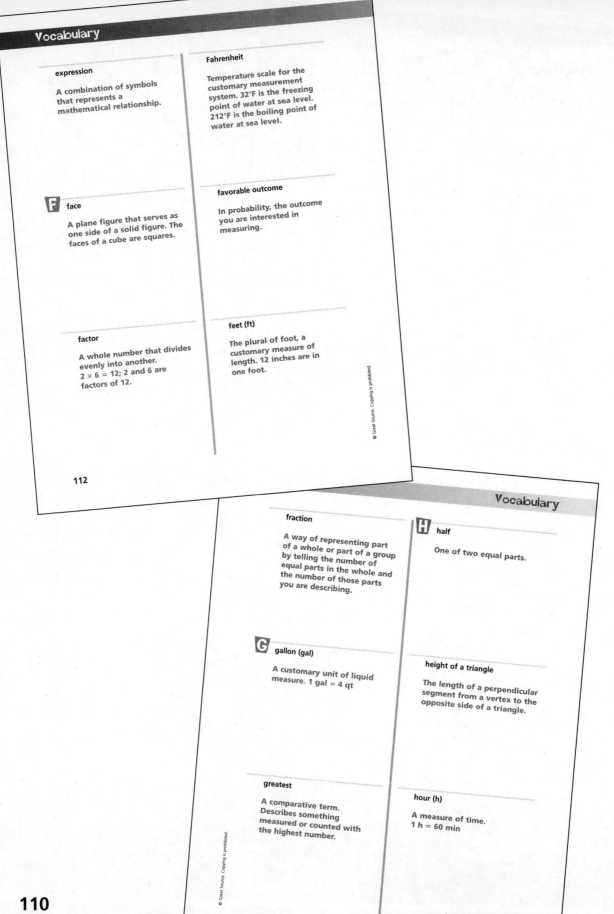

Vocabulary

expression

A combination of symbols that represents a mathematical relationship.

Fahrenheit

Temperature scale for the customary measurement system. 32°F is the freezing point of water at sea level. 212°F is the boiling point of water at sea level.

F **face**

A plane figure that serves as one side of a solid figure. The faces of a cube are squares.

favorable outcome

In probability, the outcome you are interested in measuring.

factor

A whole number that divides evenly into another.
$2 \times 6 = 12$; 2 and 6 are factors of 12.

feet (ft)

The plural of foot, a customary measure of length. 12 inches are in one foot.

112

Vocabulary

fraction

A way of representing part of a whole or part of a group by telling the number of equal parts in the whole and the number of those parts you are describing.

H **half**

One of two equal parts.

G **gallon (gal)**

A customary unit of liquid measure. 1 gal = 4 qt

height of a triangle

The length of a perpendicular segment from a vertex to the opposite side of a triangle.

greatest

A comparative term. Describes something measured or counted with the highest number.

hour (h)

A measure of time.
1 h = 60 min

K kilogram (kg)

A unit of weight or mass in the metric system; a textbook weighs about 1 kilogram.

line

An unending set of points forming a straight path extending in 2 directions.

L least

A comparative term. Describes something measured or counted with the lowest number.

line graph

A graph that connects data points to show change over time.

length of a rectangle

Usually the measure of the longest side of the rectangle.

line plot

A diagram showing frequency of data on a number line.

114

line segment

A part of a line defined by two endpoints.

median

When the numbers are arranged from least to greatest, the middle number of a set of numbers, or the mean of two middle numbers when the set has two middle numbers.

M maximum

The greatest value.

mean

A number found by dividing the sum of two or more addends by the number of addends.

meter (m)

The basic unit of length in the metric system. The width of a doorway is about 1 meter.

115

mile (mi)

A customary unit of distance.
1 mi = 5280 ft

minimum

The least value.

miles per hour (mph)

A rate of speed indicated by
the number of miles that can
be traveled at that rate in
one hour.

minute (min)

A measure of time; $\frac{1}{60}$ hour.
1 min = 60 sec

million

1,000,000

mode

The number that appears
most frequently in a set of
numbers. There may be one,
more than one, or no mode.

116

multiple

The product of a whole
number and any other whole
number.

O **outcome**

One of the possible events in
a probability situation.

N **numeral**

A symbol (not a variable)
used to represent a number.

outlier

A number in a set of data
that is much larger or smaller
than most of the other
numbers in the set.

numerator

The number that tells how
many equal parts are
described by a fraction.
In $\frac{3}{5}$, the numerator is 3.

P **pentagonal**

Describing a polygon with
5 sides.

112

117

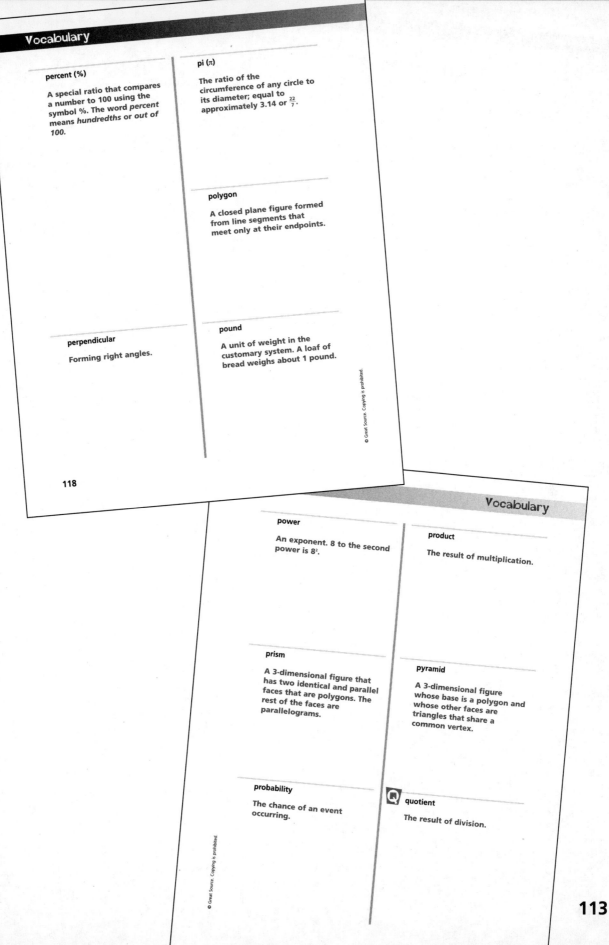

Vocabulary

percent (%)

A special ratio that compares a number to 100 using the symbol %. The word *percent* means *hundredths* or *out of 100*.

pi (π)

The ratio of the circumference of any circle to its diameter; equal to approximately 3.14 or $\frac{22}{7}$.

polygon

A closed plane figure formed from line segments that meet only at their endpoints.

perpendicular

Forming right angles.

pound

A unit of weight in the customary system. A loaf of bread weighs about 1 pound.

118

power

An exponent. 8 to the second power is 8^2.

product

The result of multiplication.

prism

A 3-dimensional figure that has two identical and parallel faces that are polygons. The rest of the faces are parallelograms.

pyramid

A 3-dimensional figure whose base is a polygon and whose other faces are triangles that share a common vertex.

probability

The chance of an event occurring.

quotient

The result of division.

119

R range

The difference between the greatest and the least value in a set of data.

right angle

An angle that measures exactly 90°.

ratio

A comparison of two numbers or measures using division.

round a number

Find the value of a number to the nearest given place value.

rectangular

Describing a polygon with 4 sides and 4 right angles.

S semi-

half

120

side of a polygon

A line segment connected to other segments to form a polygon.

square mile (mi²)

The area of a square that is exactly 1 mile on each side.

speed

A rate comparing a measure of length to a measure of time.

stem-and-leaf plot

A way of organizing information so that the numbers themselves make the display. The stems (usually tens digits) go on a vertical line from least to greatest and the leaves are the ones digits.

square

A parallelogram with four congruent sides and four right angles.

114

sum

The result of addition.

three-dimensional

Having length, width and height.

survey

A way to collect data by asking questions.

ton (t)

A customary unit of weight. 1t = 2000 lb

T **tally chart**

A way to keep track of the number of things being counted by making a tally mark for each occurrence.

triangular

Describing a polygon with 3 sides.

V **Venn diagram**

A drawing that shows relationships among sets of objects.

W **week**

A unit of time equal to 7 days.

vertex of a pyramid

The point on a pyramid where three or more triangular faces meet.

weight

A measure of the heaviness of an object. Weight varies with the pull of gravity.

volume

The number of cubic units it takes to fill a solid.

width of a rectangle

Usually the shorter dimension of a rectangle.

115

Name _____ Date _____

1. In this chapter, you're taking an imaginary trip to what country?

   _____

2. Who is inviting you to go to this country?_____

3. Why do we suspect that workers from ancient Egypt carried very heavy things?

   _____

4. Why are so many things from ancient Egypt well-preserved and not rotted away?

   _____

5. What name is given to people who study ancient civilizations by searching through ancient ruins?

   _____

6. Look at the pots shown on page 1. How do we know these pots were used for baking bread?

   _____

7. What was more important than a palace to an ancient Egyptian king?

   _____

8. What structure was used as a tomb for an ancient Egyptian king?

   _____

9. What are the steps in the four-step problem-solving method?

   _____

10. Which problem-solving step will you practice in Chapter 1?

    _____

Name _____ Date _____

1. Which continent will you visit in this chapter? _____

2. What will you do while you are there?

    _____

3. Name three things you will see on the safari.

    _____

    _____

    _____

4. What is Swahili? _____

5. What is the meaning of the Swahili word *safari*? _____

6. What is the meaning of the Swahili word *jambo*? _____

7. What are *kopjes*?

    _____

8. When a lion pride is being studied, who gives each lion its name?
    When?

    _____

9. If a lion has been given the name MKL, what does that name mean?

    _____

    _____

10. Is it possible for a lion to climb a tree? _____

11. Which problem-solving step will you practice in Chapter 2? _____

Name _____ Date _____

1. Who is inviting you to travel to Alaska? _____

2. In Alaska, you will be helping to make a film. What will be the film's topic?

   _____

3. You will travel back in time. To what month and year will you go back?

   _____

4. The Athabascan Indians called their island hunting ground *Haiditarod*.
   What does that word mean?

   _____

5. Why is this famous race called the *Iditarod*?

   _____

6. What award did Robert Sorlie win in 2003? _____

7. What was Robert Sorlie's prize in 2003?

   _____

8. Where does the race begin and end?

   _____

9. The race is always more than x miles long. What is the value of x?

   _____

10. What is the minimum number of veterinarians at each checkpoint?

    _____

11. Which problem-solving steps will you practice in Chapter 3?

    _____

Name _____ Date _____

1. What planet will the winner of the contest visit? _____

2. How will the winner of the contest travel?

   _____

3. What do you need to do to enter the contest?

   _____

4. Why is Mars called the red planet?

   _____

5. When was Mars first seen through a telescope?

   _____

6. Who was the first person to see Mars through a telescope?

   _____

7. The largest volcano in the solar system is on Mars. Use the map and the letter clues to find its name.

   ____ ____ ____ _M_ ____ _U_ ____   ____ _O_ ____ ____

8. Two Mars Rovers were launched in mid-2003. What were the dates?

   _____

9. Which two problem-solving steps will you practice in Chapter 4?

   _____

Name _____ Date _____

1. What company is planning a book about volcanoes?

    _____

2. What is the company looking for someone to do?

    _____

3. What are the four layers that make up the earth?

    _____

4. What is the approximate temperature of the mantle? _____

5. What causes a volcano to erupt?

    _____

6. Where does the word *volcano* come from?

    _____

7. Is there always a warning before a volcano erupts? _____

8. What was the date of the 1980 eruption of Mount St. Helens?

    _____

9. Which problem-solving step will you practice in Chapter 5?

    _____

Name _____ **Date** _____

1. What is the name of the ranch you will be visiting?

   _____

2. What four things can you learn to do at Lazy R Horse Ranch?

   _____

3. In which century was the Pony Express used to deliver messages?

   _____

4. Who painted *Coming and Going of the Pony Express*?

   _____

5. What important role did workhorses play in history?

   _____

   _____

6. Where does the term *horsepower* come from?

   _____

7. In this chapter you will practice all four problem-solving steps.
   What are the four steps?

   _____

8. Have you ever helped take care of a horse? Do you think it would be a
   lot of work? Explain.

   _____

   _____

   _____

   _____

Name _____ Date _____

Fill in the circle with the letter of the correct answer.

1. Which of these figures is a pyramid?

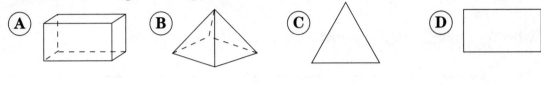

   Ⓐ   Ⓑ   Ⓒ   Ⓓ

2. Which of the following is *not* an odd number?

   Ⓐ   5   Ⓑ   19   Ⓒ   17   Ⓓ   4

3. Which of the shaded figures is *not* the base of the pyramid?

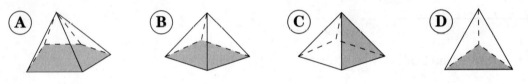

   Ⓐ   Ⓑ   Ⓒ   Ⓓ

For exercises 4–6, mark the letter of the group of words that means the same as the underlined words.

4. The truck weighed <u>at least 2 tons</u>.

   Ⓐ   4,000 pounds or more   Ⓒ   400 pounds or more

   Ⓑ   4,000 pounds or less   Ⓓ   400 pounds or less

5. After the party, there were <u>over a dozen</u> muffins left over.

   Ⓐ   fewer than 12   Ⓒ   about 13

   Ⓑ   more than 10   Ⓓ   13 or more

6. The puppy weighed <u>1.5 pounds</u>.

   Ⓐ   15 pounds   Ⓒ   one and one-half pounds

   Ⓑ   one and one-fifth pound   Ⓓ   one and one-fifth pounds

For exercises 7–8, fill in the circle with the letter of the correct answer. Explain why you made your choice.

7. In these sentences, which number is an estimate?

   One dollar is worth the same as 5 dimes and 2 quarters.

   Lunch will cost about 3 dollars.

   (A) One   _____

   (B) 5   _____

   (C) 2   _____

   (D) 3   _____

8. There are two seventh-grade classes. Each class has 28 students. Which picture best shows the math in the sentence?

   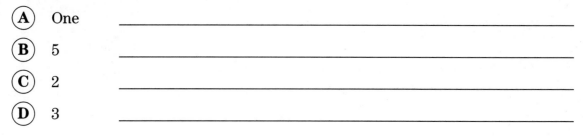

   (A)   _____

          _____

   (B)   _____

          _____

For exercise 9, write your answer on the lines provided.

9. Melanie has 2 more bracelets than her sister Josie. Write a sentence using words, numerals, and symbols, that has the same meaning.

   _____

For exercise 10, draw a picture to show the math.

10. The carpet was 12 feet long and 10 feet wide.

Name _____ Date _____

Fill in the circle with the letter of the correct answer.

1. According to the circle graph, which of these statements is *not* true?

   Band Members

   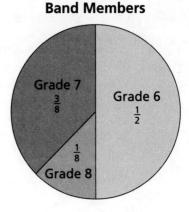

   (A) Less than half of the band members are in grade 7.

   (B) Half of the band members are in grade 6.

   (C) Less than a quarter of the band members are in grade 8.

   (D) More of the band members are in grade 8 than in any other grade.

2. On which days were fewer than 25 students present in Room 109?

   (A) Monday, Tuesday, and Wednesday

   (B) Monday and Wednesday

   (C) Thursday and Friday

   (D) Monday, Wednesday, and Friday

   This Week's Attendance Room 109

   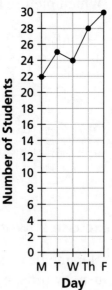

3. Mario's family had a birthday party for his grandmother, who was turning 85. How many people were at the party?

   (A) 29

   (B) 23

   (C) 15

   (D) 8

   Ages of People at Party

0	2 3
1	5 6 8 9 9
2	0 1 1 4
3	1 1 2
4	0 1 4
5	2 7
6	1 4 5 7 9
7	2 3
8	5 6 9

   Key: 1|5 = 15 years old

124

Name _____ Date _____

For exercise 4, fill in the circle with the letter of the correct answer and explain why you made your choice.

4. Use the stem-and-leaf plot from exercise 3. What was the median age of the people at the family reunion?

(**A**) 87 _____

(**B**) 40 _____

(**C**) 89 _____

(**D**) 44 _____

For exercises 5–7, write your answers on the lines provided.

5. The parking lot opens at 7:00 A.M. By 9:00 A.M. every space is taken. There are 18 rows of cars. Each row has the same number of cars. How many cars are in the lot? To solve the problem, what additional information do you need?

_____

6. Rachel was born on October 20, 1992. How old was she in 2003? What additional information do you need to solve the problem?

_____

7. Write four things this bar graph tells you about the seventh grade students at Diamond Middle School.

_____

_____

_____

_____

_____

_____

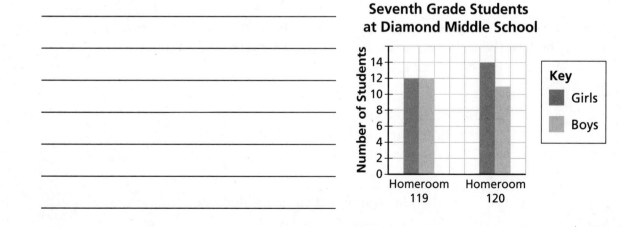

Seventh Grade Students at Diamond Middle School

Key
■ Girls
■ Boys

Name _____ Date _____

Fill in the circle with the letter of the correct answer.

1. Mrs. Chang bought 3 bags of apples. Each bag had 8 apples. To find the total number of apples, which picture could you use?

   (A) 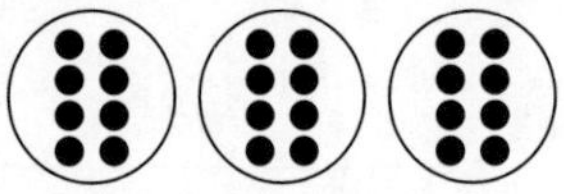 ⬤⬤⬤ (B) 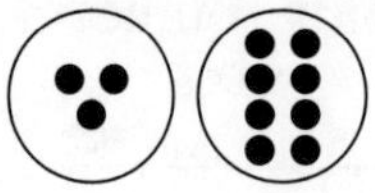 ⬤⬤ (C) 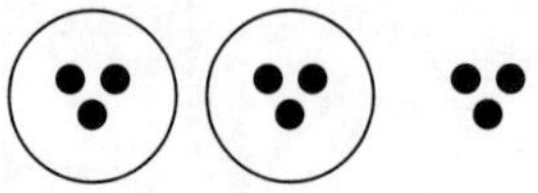 ⬤ ⬤ ⬤

2. One fifth of the 20 students on the middle school track team are boys. Which picture could you use to find the number of boys on the middle school track team?

   (A) 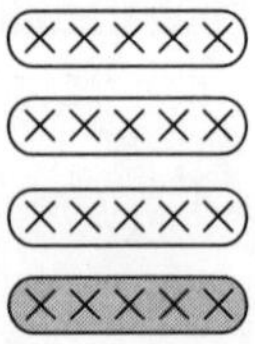 ⨂⨂⨂⨂⨂ (B) 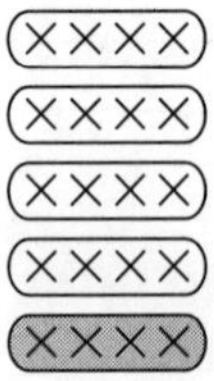 ⨂⨂⨂⨂ (C)  ×××⨂××××××××××××××××××××

3. Carly ran 4 miles. Her older sister Kerri ran $2\frac{1}{2}$ times as far. Which picture could you use to find the distance Kerri ran?

   (A) 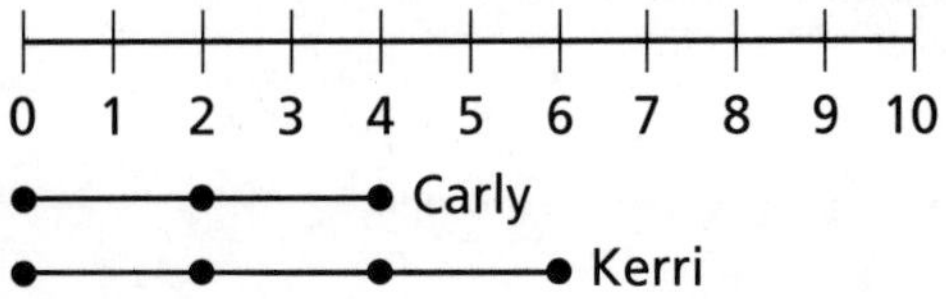 ├─┼─┼─┼─┼─┼─┼─┼─┼─┼─┤
       0 1 2 3 4 5 6 7 8 9 10
       ●───●───● Carly
       ●───●───●───● Kerri

   (B) 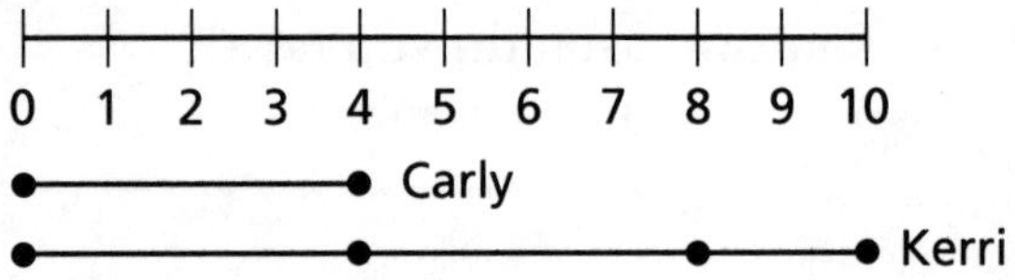 ├─┼─┼─┼─┼─┼─┼─┼─┼─┼─┤
       0 1 2 3 4 5 6 7 8 9 10
       ●───────● Carly
       ●───────────────● Kerri

4. Charlene turned 14 on September 13, 2003. Which expression would you use to find the year Charlene was born?

   (A) $2003 + 14$ (B) $2003 - 14$ (C) $2003 + 13$ (D) $2003 - 13$

5. Mr. Randall drove 155 miles in 5 hours. Which expression would you use to find his average speed in miles per hour?

   (A) $155 + 5$ (B) $155 - 5$ (C) 155×5 (D) $155 \div 5$

6. There are 25 students in Mr. Carlson's class. Twelve of them are girls. Which of the following tells how to find the fraction of students in Mr. Carlson's class that are boys?

   (A) **Plan A**
   - Subtract 12 from 25.
   - Use that difference as the numerator.
   - Use 25 as the denominator.

   (B) **Plan B**
   - Use 12 as the numerator and 25 as the denominator.

126

Name _____ Date _____

Choose the letter of the best answer, then write why you made that choice.

7. Harold took 4 spelling tests. His scores were 90, 82, 85, 80, and 85.
   Which plan tells how to find Harold's mean score?

   (A) **Plan A**

   - Add the scores.   _____

   - Divide the sum by 5.   _____

   (B) **Plan B**   _____

   - Order the scores least to greatest.   _____

   - Use the middle score.   _____

Write the plan you would use to answer the question.

8. Out of the 50 students in the band, 3 missed the concert. How would
   you find the percent of students in the band that missed the concert?

   Plan

   _____

   _____

   _____

   _____

Write a math word problem that could be solved by using this plan.

9. **Plan**
   - Multiply $4.50 by 3.
   - Subtract the product from $20.00.

   _____

   _____

   _____

   _____

Name _____ Date _____

Fill in the circle with the letter of the correct answer.

1. Lucy answers 7 out of 10 questions correctly. Which equation would you use to find the fraction of the questions Lucy answered incorrectly?

   (A) $\frac{10}{10} - \frac{7}{10} = \frac{3}{10}$ **(C)** $10 - 3 = 7$

   (B) $\frac{10}{10} - \frac{3}{10} = \frac{7}{10}$ **(D)** $10 - 7 = 3$

For exercises 2–5, fill in the circle with the letter of the correct answer. Write your plan in the box.

2. Terry was present on 4 out of the 5 school days this week. What percent of the days was she present?

   (A) 40%   **(C)** 80%

   (B) 20%   **(D)** 60%

3. Shawn's birthday is on April 29. Henri's birthday is 5 days later. When is Henri's birthday?

   (A) May 4   **(C)** April 34

   (B) May 5   **(D)** May 6

4. Heidi weighs 78 pounds. Her cat weighs 8 pounds. If Heidi stands on the scale holding her cat, what weight will be shown on the scale?

   (A) 70 pounds   **(C)** 78 pounds

   (B) 86 pounds   **(D)** 788 pounds

5. A choral group has 50 students. Two fifths of them are boys. How many students in the choral group are boys?

   (A) 30 students   **(C)** 50 students

   (B) 45 students   **(D)** 20 students

Fill in the circle with the letter of the correct answer. Explain why you made your choice.

6. A truck weighs 5,000 pounds. Which word expression describes how to write 5000 pounds as tons?

   (A) 5,000 pounds ÷ 2,000 pounds per ton _____

   (B) 5,000 pounds × 2,000 pounds per ton _____

7. A box is 40 inches long and 15 inches wide. It is $\frac{1}{2}$ as deep as it is long. Which word expression describes how to find the volume of the box?

   (A) 40 inches × 15 inches × 20 inches _____

   (B) 40 inches × 15 inches × 40 inches _____

   (C) 40 inches × 15 inches × 30 inches _____

   (D) 40 inches × 15 inches × 7 1\2 inches _____

For exercises 8–9, write your answer on the lines.

8. Mr. Chang bought a used car that cost $12,400. The dealer deducted $2500 from the price because Mr. Chang traded in his old car. How much did Mr. Chang pay? Show your work.

   _____

   _____

9. Ellen plans to go away to soccer camp. The camp will last 27 days. She wants to know how many weeks that is. Ellen's work is at the right.

   What did Ellen do wrong? Show how you would find the exact number of weeks.

   _____

   _____

   _____

   _____

Ellen
```
   27
 X 7
-----
  189
```

Name _____ Date _____

Fill in the circle with the letter of the correct answer.

1. You correctly find the volume of a suitcase. Which of the following would label your answer?

   (A) square feet

   (B) cubic feet

   (C) feet

   (D) pounds

2. The length of a photo is $1\frac{2}{3}$ times its width. The photo is 3 inches wide. Which of the following best describes the length of the photo?

   (A) 3 inches

   (B) less than 3 inches

   (C) more than 3 inches

   (D) none of these

3. Naomi drove home at an average speed of 25 miles per hour. Which of the following is true about her speed in miles per minute?

   (A) It is 25 miles per minute.

   (B) It is more than 25 miles per minute.

   (C) It is less than 25 miles per minute.

   (D) none of these

4. A pizza has a diameter of 12 inches. Which unit best labels the area of the pizza?

   (A) inches

   (B) square inches

   (C) cubic inches

   (D) none of these

5. Emily makes handbags out of duct tape. If she makes 9 bags in 4 days, how many bags per day does she average? (**HINT:** Use estimation to choose the most reasonable answer.)

   (A) 2.25 bags per day

   (B) 225 bags per day

   (C) 0.225 bags per day

   (D) 22.5 bags per day

Name _____ Date _____

Fill in the circle with the letter of the correct answer. Tell why you made your choice.

6. A circular rug has a radius of 4 feet. What is the area of the rug?
   (**HINT:** Use estimation to choose the most reasonable answer.)

   Ⓐ 5024 square fee   _____

   Ⓑ 502.4 square feet   _____

   Ⓒ 5.024 square feet   _____

   Ⓓ 50.24 square feet   _____

For exercises 7–9, write the answer on the lines provided.

7. Alaska has an area of 663,267 square miles. Texas has an area of 268,581 square miles. Write an expression that describes an estimate of the difference between the two areas.

   _____

8. A rope is 247 inches long. About how many feet long is it?
   Show your work.

   _____

9. Describe two ways you can look back at the solution to a problem to check it.

   _____

   _____

   _____

   _____

   _____

Name _____ Date _____

Exercises 1–8 are about this problem.

Gen rides her bike to school 3 days each week. The front wheel on her bike has a diameter of 2 feet. When she rides from her house to school, her front wheel goes around 725 times. About how much less than a mile does Gen live from school?

For exercise 1–3, fill in the circle with the letter of the correct answer.

1. Which information from the problem is not needed to solve the problem?

   (A) Gen rides her bike to school 3 days each week.

   (B) The front wheel on her bike has a diameter of 2 feet.

   (C) When she rides from her house to school, her front wheel goes around 725 times.

2. Which additional information is *not* needed to solve the problem?

   (A) There are 5280 feet in a mile.

   (B) There are 3 feet in a yard.

   (C) The value of π is approximately 3.14.

3. Which of the following best shows *a bike wheel that has a diameter of 2 feet*?

   (A) 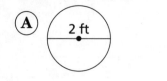   (B)   (C)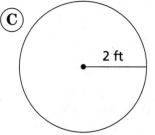

4. Fill in numbers to complete the plan that could be used to solve the original problem.

   Plan

   • Find the circumference of the tire: Multiply _____ by _____.

   • Multiply the circumference of the tire by _____.

   • Subtract the product from _____.

5. Carry out the plan from exercise 4.

6. Write a sentence that gives the correct answer to the original problem. Be sure to include the units with the number.

_____

7. Explain how you could use estimation to check that the distance from Gen's house to school that you calculated makes sense.

_____

_____

8. What are the four problem-solving steps? Choose one of the steps. Tell why you think that step is important.

_____

_____

_____

_____

_____

_____

_____

_____

_____

_____

_____